# The insiders guide to advertising

## How the business of advertising really works

CRAIG MAWDSLEY & BRIDGET ANGEAR

THE CHOIR PRESS

First published in the United Kingdom in 2021 by
The Choir Press

ISBN 978-1-78963-193-7

# Contents

# Introduction

This book aims to give you a flavour of the advertising industry as we enter the third decade of the twenty-first century. Advertising is an industry that's a few hundred years old, but an activity that has been with us since the dawn of civilisation. Recent years have brought dramatic change, as the internet has both created new possibilities and threatened the fabric of the entire ad industry. It has driven explosive growth in the reach and commercial value of advertising whilst shaking apart the established structures that deliver it. This is a fascinating time to reflect on the state of advertising.

Whilst there are academic and theoretical foundations to the study of advertising, this is a book mainly informed by over twenty-five years of personal experience in advertising agencies, with exposure to all the other players in the industry, in many countries. We have seen and done a lot, but of course not everything, so there will be omissions. And in an industry constantly in thrall to the next new thing, trends in advertising just emerging will not have made it in. As we write, everyone is talking about Tik Tok; it was barely mentioned when we began writing this book.

But the fundamentals of the industry endure. They have for the past twenty-five years, for hundreds of years before that and most likely for hundreds of years to come. This book focuses on those fundamentals, rather than the superficial changes that swirl around them.

Advertising is an activity that has shaped society as much as it has shaped business and is a fascinating and exhilarating discipline to work in and study. Whether you have a casual interest, are considering studying advertising, or even making a career of it, we hope this book will arm you with the most important aspects to consider when approaching the advertising industry.

**Chapter 1**

# Advertising is everywhere

Where there are people, there is advertising.

It might be obvious, like the bright lights and video screens of Tokyo, commercial messages demanding attention all around.

It might be simpler and more handmade, with a photocopied piece of paper taped on the side of a building in Sao Paolo asking about a lost dog.

The 2 billion active Facebook users, or 1.9 billion who watch YouTube videos every month (or their Chinese equivalents, Weibo, WeChat, Youku) have no need even to leave the house, as the smartphone has now become a ubiquitous personalised advertising delivery system.

Advertising is everywhere and has always been with us in its simplest form of words and pictures containing persuasive ideas.

Advertising is the most visible form of capitalism, attracting criticism from those who dislike commerce, and is blamed for many ills of modern society. It is simultaneously dismissed as ineffective nonsense and endowed with magical powers. Even in the most liberal societies it is constrained and regulated to some extent.

Within the advertising industry itself, articles and books periodically claim the death of advertising, and those who work in advertising go to great lengths to avoid even using the word, for fear it will make them sound marginal or old fashioned.

It is a powerful force in business and a huge global industry, worth in excess of half a trillion dollars. Advertising is in growth almost everywhere in the world. Without the advertising industry, the modern world would be very different. The influence, size and continued growth of Google and Facebook is due almost entirely to advertising. The broader effect of both these corporations (and their Chinese equivalents) on society, culture and politics is thanks to advertising. In many ways, Google and Facebook are the advertising industry, accounting for almost all the growth and a huge percentage of the spend in most countries.

There has never been a more interesting time to understand the role that advertising plays for people, business and society.

## Defining advertising

First, we need to define what we talk about when we talk about advertising. Advertising is a surprisingly broad and elusive concept, used interchangeably in English as verb and noun.

The broadest definition of advertising is as a verb – 'to make something known or draw attention to something'. There is no assumed or explicit intent at this broad and simple level; it is just about promoting information.

The Oxford English Dictionary defines advertising as to 'describe or draw attention to (a product, service or event) in a public medium in order to promote sales or attendance'. To the uninitiated this looks like an adequate and comprehensive definition. But it does not take much thought to see how this fails as a practical definition when trying to understand the advertising industry. The concept of attention is problematic (as it turns out, attention is by no means required for advertising to work – not active attention at least), and this definition also seems to rule out any 'advertising' done in the public sector or for charitable organisations.

We need to think more broadly to define the modern practice of advertising.

The economic theory of perfect competition, first defined in the 19th century by Leon Walras, has perfect information as a vital component part. The idea is that, for economic theory to work, we must assume that everyone making decisions does so with complete knowledge of all the options. Advertising plays a role in this in the real world, providing the information that enables people to make better decisions. Economies work better the more information there is. Available resources flow to the option that provides the most utility for the price the market is willing to pay. When information is less well distributed, people make less-informed decisions and the available resources in the market fail to flow to the best ideas. There is not enough time or energy for everyone to try every option in a market, so advertising acts as a proxy to find out which one might be best for them.

In practice, advertising is about much more than infor-mation, at least in the rational sense. Often the intent of advertising is to add intangible value to the product or service itself. In the increasing absence of rational, tangible advantage, advertising manufactures emotional advantage for brands. Some brands just make you feel better than others. At this point economists start to find it very hard to incorporate advertising in their models. Think of a market where most of the products perform in a very similar way. It is no good telling people yours is better (and probably not legal to do so), because it is not true. Instead you try to make it seem more attractive in a more emotional way, associating it with a particular lifestyle or giving the product an appealing 'personality' that people want to spend time with (personality in advertising is created through characterful use of words, pictures and design to communicate a feeling – it's not what is said, but how it is said). We can illustrate this by thinking of a product sector (fragrance is always a good example) where there is very little rational 'information' that would enable you to choose one over another. The role of the advertising in this case is to create intangible value that stimulates desire, often by associating the fragrance with an attractive celebrity. In the case of alcoholic drinks, or clothing, the advertising helps to build a set of shared values that are used to project status to others. This is one of the roles a brand can play. If everyone knows the cost or ethos of a particular brand, that brand can be used to send signals to others. A shared belief that Guinness is drunk by people with strength of character is a valuable thing for those who want to communicate that about themselves. Guinness' advertising idea 'Made Of More' is designed to do precisely this. This role of advertising in creating shared meaning is a critical part of its power and the value it creates.

To the rational mind, this may sound like total nonsense. But we do make many, or perhaps even most of, our decisions based on nonsense. Neuroscience has demonstrated that every decision the brain makes is emotional and instinctive to some degree. In *Descartes' Error*, Antonio Damasio demonstrated that emotions always guide decision-making, citing the case of Phineas Gage, an unfortunate railroad worker who lost part of his brain in an accident at work. The damaged area of the brain was the part responsible for processing emotion, and in a surprising side effect, this left Phineas unable to make even the simplest decisions. Whilst the details of the case have been disputed, the idea has common currency in the ad industry and advertising that accesses emotions has often been proven to create more powerful effects. Even in cultures where people try to adopt a highly rational 'face' when talking about advertising (Germany springs to mind), there's still a lot of perfume sold. It's always emotional.

From here comes the idea that advertising might be lying. That celebrity has been paid to appear in that ad; they haven't chosen to use that product or service themselves, and even if they had, the advertising is 'lying' when it implies that the viewer could somehow be like them by purchasing it. A Nespresso machine in the kitchen will not summon George Clooney to the doorstep. Advertising uses the power of words, sounds and images to manipulate the brain. The brain is constantly trying to make sense of the world around, to tell ourselves a story about what's happening. In this sense all human cognition is a lie. This particular critique of advertising is based on an assumed intent of the industry – to make people feel dissatisfied with their lives so they buy things they do not 'need'.

Advertising became a more pervasive influence and played a bigger role in business and culture in the second half of the twentieth century when (in Europe and North America at least) the capacity to produce goods and services exceeded simple need. Incomes increased so that most households could cover basic needs and became ready and able to discover new experiences and lifestyles. Advertising offered different ways to achieve social and individual progress – new ways to live, new things to try, new identities to assume. None of these new possibilities was about basic need, so advertising was required to make them attractive, helping to fuel capitalist economies across the world.

It is very hard to disentangle advertising from this broader role of capitalism in culture. Where, for example, should the conceptual line be drawn between advertising and retail? The displays in shop windows tempt us to buy, and in some way, they are advertising. Seeing someone drive past in a new BMW might make the driver of a different brand of car feel a little less satisfied with their current mode of transport. Seeing James Bond check the time on his Omega watch in a movie might make users of other timepieces feel a little less than adequate. None of these things are 'advertising' exactly, but they are all part of the system of selling.

Advertising also plays a role in non-capitalist societies. There are fewer of these around nowadays, but the North Korean regime is just as interested as the Soviet regime used to be in harnessing the power of words, music and images to make their citizens think and feel certain things. There appears to be quite a high information content in the advertising produced in these places, perhaps giving you numbers about industrial production or productivity. But it is invariably communicated in the context of heroic images of the people or the leader. It is advertising. It is designed to make people feel happy about their lives, so they don't question the behaviour of the government. Sometimes we call that propaganda (information that is actively and intentionally designed to mislead). The mural on the side of the North Korean tractor factory is designed to make its workers feel like heroes playing their role in building a socialist utopia. If you believe those workers are being deliberately misled, and are making decisions that are against their interests (because they would be better off wanting different things, producing better tractors, or feeling dissatisfied with their lifestyle and over-throwing their government), then it's propaganda. But if the advertising makes them happy, then who are we to say that it is a bad thing? What is the difference between advertising and propaganda? Simply the value judgement of the person using the word.

A more specific definition of advertising is 'paid-for messaging designed to achieve a commercial outcome'. We could define it by this specific intent – to part people from their money. But even this is problematic (for one thing, it rules out much of the advertising that wins creative awards, more of which later). A lot of advertising is dedicated to making people feel something different about a charitable cause, a social issue, or to change their behaviour as citizens, rather than shape their spending as consumers.

Perhaps the law can offer guidance. US law (including Federal Trade Commission and Lanham Acts) defines advertising as 'the act or practice of attracting public notice and attention. It includes all forms of public announcement that are intended to aid directly or indirectly in the furtherance or promulgation of an idea, or in directing attention to a business, commodity, service or entertainment'. This captures something essential in understanding the advertising industry – the concept of the 'idea'. These 'ideas' are not academic, philosophical, profound or world changing, and can often be criticised as derivative or banal. But they are ideas nonetheless, ideas about the life people might be able to lead, views they should agree with, causes they might care about. Coca Cola spent many years equating their drink with happiness and Pepsi with the rising energy of the next generation. Dove is campaigning for real beauty. Apple encourages people to Think Different. Wal-Mart tells people that if they save money, they can live better. Mastercard wants people to consider experiences to be priceless.

Advertising is about ideas (although not entirely about attention). And those ideas are being promoted with a specific agenda in mind. For the purpose of this book we will be defining advertising as *the promotion of ideas with commercial, benevolent or political intent.*

Advertising is words, music, images or combinations thereof, produced with a clear agenda in mind. To paraphrase Hamlet, the intent is the thing. It is not art for art's sake; it is there to make you think, feel or do something. It has been promoted by the organisation that wants to create that thought, feeling or behaviour. There may be commercial intent, benevolent intent, or the search for political power, but it is this intent that makes it advertising.

Whether that intent is considered positive or malign is down to your personal views, but without turning the clock back on society and technology, it is pretty much impossible to have no advertising at all. Advertising is always the expression of some type of power, and the amount of money you have to spend on advertising makes the effect more powerful. Only those with money, connections or extraordinary creativity can use the power of advertising to achieve their intent and this makes it problematic for some: advertising can help to reinforce existing power structures in business and society, crowding out new ideas and stifling change, although there is always the possibility of renegade creativity disrupting this.

## The meaning of advertising in the advertising industry

The word 'advertising' has a very specific meaning within the industry itself. It was once an unambiguous and attractive term. In recent years, the word itself has fallen out of favour, in a way that must be baffling for those outside the industry.

The first cracks in the lexicography came during the ascendancy of direct marketing and the emergence of direct marketing specialists both agency and client side. Advertising was something that happened in broadcast media (the channels that have no direct return path for the audience, like TV or posters), with no expectation of direct response. This is sometimes referred to as 'one-to-many' communication in contrast to 'one-to-one' communication. Direct marketing expected a proportion of the audience to pick up the phone, or send a coupon through the post, to receive the product or service directly or have a conversation with a salesperson. Advertising created entertaining and attractive images, films or soundtracks, whilst direct marketing was heavy with information and inducements to act. Advertising was indirect, hard to pin down and occasionally self-indulgent and unaccountable; direct marketing was plain in intent and generated measurable sales.

An industry grew around direct marketing that eroded the influence of the advertising agency with marketing departments. The word 'advertising' was now used to describe only a part of the ad industry. Those working in advertising agencies became coy about using the word, fearing that it made them seem marginal, wasteful, and worst of all, old fashioned. Instead they became 'branding agencies' or 'marketing agencies' or 'ideas companies' in the 'creative industries'. This continues to the point where an uninformed observer would find it hard to work out what everyone is actually doing.

This confusion became worse with the arrival of digital technology and the rise of the 'digital agency', claiming to know things that 'advertising agencies' do not. Marketing professionals will perhaps always continue to worry that they do not know enough about the latest new thing. Changes in technology and the new cultures and behaviours that come along with them always require a change in mindset, along with an understanding of particular technical specifications for message delivery. You can argue that 'digital' is a redundant signifier as everything is now digital in some way, but digital agencies continue to exist and thrive. In this context, the word 'advertising' is assumed to refer to channels and formats that existed before the internet, excluding the bulk of the current advertising industry (Google and Facebook). As a result, 'advertising' agencies would by definition be marginal and trapped in the past. Not a nice idea.

'Advertising' is also out of favour as a noun. In discussion between client and agency, or otherwise within the industry, it is much more in vogue to use the word 'idea' (an even less defined and more elusive concept, but somehow more attractive as a result). This is because it is more valuable for clients to have ideas that can be used across a range of channels and over time. Any individual advertisement will only have a small effect. It will only reach a percentage of the relevant audience for a small amount of time, so it is of some use, but only as part of a broader advertising campaign. At the height of mass media, a single advertisement in a single channel could reach almost everyone. This is no longer true. Consistency over time is also very important. Brands are stronger when they turn up looking the same and saying the same things in the same places to the same people for a long time. Each message reinforces the last and everyone gets a clear and settled view of what that brand means (brand 'meaning' is about how quickly and easily a feeling is generated in the brain when you are exposed to a brand; if it happens quickly, that brand is much more likely to be chosen). Adverts are only the output of that process. The idea that sits behind the advertising is much more important.

In the advertising industry, the phrase 'it's just advertising' is often used to criticise creative work that is perceived to lack ambition, innovation and longevity. Ideas have much greater influence than adverts. At their best, advertisements are idea-delivery systems, but the power comes from the idea. If it is a very good and influential idea it will change many of the things the organisation says and does, reaching way beyond the advertisements.

When agencies go to great lengths to avoid using the word 'advertising', it is partly because they want to do more than just make adverts. In the past, before other disciplines intervened, the advertising agency had great influence in the companies that procured their services, often with direct access to the chief executive officer, not just the chief marketing officer. Agencies had an advisory role that was much broader than the adverts they made. This had business benefits for advertising agencies (often associated with higher fees), but it was also about power and influence, as they helped make big decisions with big consequences. If the job of the agency is simply to execute other people's decisions by just making adverts, then there is much less power involved.

Advertising and brands are usually linked, but they are quite different. The brand is a conceptual idea, embodied in a set of design attributes and experiences that have intangible associations and meanings. Advertising is one of the things a brand does (and also one of the things that organisations or people that are not brands do; it is not the exclusive preserve of brands). Advertising is an activity that may be solely about building the meaning of the brand, so brands, branding and advertising are very tightly connected. But advertising does a number of other things as well. It is often designed to create action (buy a product, sign up for a service, change behaviour of citizens). Sometimes these actions might actually diminish the value of the brand, or act in contradiction to the principles of the brand. The action in the short term becomes more important than the long-term value of the brand. When the intent of advertising is to drive direct response, best practice principles of how to drive response can make many advertisements for different brands look very similar. Whilst this might not erode the value of the brand, it plays very little role in building it. Not all brands advertise, but not all advertising builds brands.

In the client organisations that commission and pay for advertising, advertising is a subset of marketing. Agencies will often tend to act as though the marketing director thinks of little other than advertising and the advertising agency, but it is just one of a wide range of activities in their responsibility. The role and importance of advertising varies dramatically by organisation and industry.

If a business exists primarily online, then advertising will be critical, and will account for a huge quantity of sales and customer acquisition, with Google and Facebook playing a big role (in most parts of the world, apart from China). Advertising is often referred to in these companies as 'acquisition' and is very close to the heart of the business. Without it, it is very hard for them to grow.

In more traditional packaged-goods companies, the sales force that deals directly with retailers is much more important than the advertising. Getting more prominent shelf space (physical or virtual) makes a much bigger difference to sales than millions spent in media. As a result, those involved in advertising can be seen as a bit wasteful, perhaps not serious businesspeople. But of course, shelf space is often secured on the promise of advertising spend to attract customers. Advertising works one way or another. In trade magazines for the packaged-goods industry, like *The Grocer* in the UK, there are many adverts whose primary objective is to advertise the advertising spend, encouraging retailers to stock the product in advance of anticipated demand.

For contract-based organisations (telecoms, financial services, utilities), Customer Relationship Management (usually abbreviated as CRM, a rather long and complex term that is probably better understood as 'service') is most important. Retaining customers and encouraging them to spend more delivers revenue and profits. Using advertising to attract new customers is an expensive business that requires retention of customers for a few years to deliver returns on the acquisition cost.

In all these examples, advertising only works as part of a sales and marketing system, promoting products and services that are widely available, at the right price. It can only work for governments if it exists within a framework of legislation and only works for charities if they are able to gather donations effectively and use them to fulfil their charitable purpose. Understanding how all these pieces fit together is critical to understand how to use advertising well.

Despite all the semantic debates about the word, the qualms about the ethics and the limitations of the effect, despite the changing tech context and the angst of existing players, advertising remains an exciting industry. Because advertising can make magical things happen – just by putting an idea into the world the fortunes of companies can be changed, the working lives of millions influenced, prosperity built, lives saved, and millions entertained.

**Key ideas:**

> Advertising can be defined in many ways but in its broadest sense is the 'promotion of ideas with commercial, benevolent or political intent'. At its best it can achieve great things for people, brands and organisations. Whilst it is rare for advertising to make things worse (despite the adage 'nothing kills a bad product faster than good advertising'), much goes by unnoticed.

*So how does advertising actually work and what is practically involved in making it happen?*

# Chapter 2
# The advertising business

All advertising was once created within businesses, charities or government departments. A design or publicity function would commission advertisements (often sponsored art-works) and then negotiate directly with publications or poster sites to get them seen.

Advertising then became more sophisticated and scientific, as Fordist division of labour set in. As in many other disciplines, the process of creating advertising campaigns was split into specialist component parts, and those who used to do the entire process themselves were replaced by teams of people specialising in just part of the process. They moved out of client companies to work in agencies, then the agencies created many departments, which in turn became separate specialist organisations enabling improved delivery and excellence in their specialism, making the whole process better over time.

The advertising industry is built from these component parts, split across different organisations with different skills and objectives. Marketing departments define business models and products or services to promote. They write the brief for agencies to create advertisements and media strategies, so people see them. Media owners build audiences whose time or space is interrupted with advertising. The advertising industry works when all these elements are well connected.

## Creating the messages.

The advertising industry is the organisation of messages searching for audiences.

Getting to a message involves a process of analysis which might take hours or years. There may be analysis of the client organisation and what it seeks to do, what competitors it may face and the advantages or disadvantages they have for the audience. This audience may also be studied, to discover what they care about, to understand the other things that compete for their attention, and the values and priorities they have in life. Or there may be none of this analysis, and instead just gut feel and presentation with confidence and panache. Different agencies will act differently, according to culture and personal beliefs. There is no one right way of doing it, no tried and tested optimised process that always delivers an effective answer. But the end product must be an idea of some sort.

Creative skill is then required to devise an interesting execution of this idea, drawing on cultural references, the latest in design thinking and language. The idea, in advertising, is the conceptual thought that drives a range of different executions appropriate to the choice of media. Ideally, this idea is flexible enough to be expressed with just a few words, and rich enough to sustain multiple expressions in multiple channels. Creative departments will often be interested in how this idea compares to other excellent advertisements that have gone before, and perhaps some data about how similar messages might have performed in the past. Once that idea is conceived then it needs to be made into advertising, working with illustrators, photographers, typographers, filmmakers, designers, coders, event managers, or whoever is required to move from notion to execution.

If all this goes well, an advertisement might be created, but this is not yet an advertising campaign. That only exists when an audience has been found.

## Finding the audience

Finding an audience requires a knowledge of channels that carry advertising (now an almost endless list and constantly changing) and reliable data about the audience of each of these channels (how many people do they reach and who are those people?). This audience then has a tacit or explicit agreement with the content provider – advertising makes the content free to consume (or substantially cheaper), so they tolerate its presence. Those who sell advertising work out a way to price the audience's time or attention and a mechanism to sell it to advertisers.

These two processes will happen at the most sophisticated or most rudimentary ends of the industry. Imagine seeing a person stand on a busy shopping street with a sign pointing at their restaurant around the corner. That was the result of a series of decisions: possibly tacit and instinctive, but decisions nonetheless. They had to decide to stand on the street with a sign versus all the other potential options. They had to work out what to put on the sign, make the sign, choose a place to stand, stand there themselves or pay someone else to do it, notice whether anyone followed the sign or not and then adjust their approach accordingly. The same decision process creates a global multimedia advertising campaign.

Most of the functions required to create and deliver advertising now happen outside the companies who make the products or services advertised. It is much easier to attract interesting talent to the varied creative challenges of agency life than it is to persuade them to work in a detergent company in a remote part of the country five days a week, for example. Finance also plays a role – why have advertising creation as part of the fixed cost base when it could be a variable cost? The extent to which services are provided in-house or bought in from external agencies varies by company and is dynamic over time, but the core players in advertising are now well established.

A range of organisations work together to create the messages (from client companies to creative agencies and a variety of production companies). Another group find the audiences (from media planning and buying agencies, through ad exchanges, and all the services and channels that carry advertising). Research is woven through both core activities, with research companies of all shapes and sizes providing a running commentary on what the audience cares about and where they are spending their time. Each of these players has different motivations and incentives; the interaction of these produces the advertising.

Client companies come in all shapes and sizes, but their defining feature is that they are only really in the advertising business as a means to another end. The creation of advertising is a small, although costly, part of what they do. They exist to sell vacuum cleaners, or run a restaurant, or make pet food, or whatever else they do. They may spend a lot of their money on advertising, but they are more like other companies in their industry that do not advertise than they are like an advertising agency. Advertising is not the core of their business, but attracting and retaining customers always is. Some are in the enviable position of having a product or service so good that people spread the word to one another, and little advertising is required. But that tends to be a very lucky business, or a normal business having a very lucky period (Google is a good example – the best product in an innovative category that had a great deal of inherent interest from almost everyone in the world, they grew rapidly, with virtually no advertising apart from the product itself, although now when they enter adjacent categories like smartphones, advertising plays a much bigger role). For most other organisations, it's generally a never-ending war for attention and regard. Advertising is a powerful weapon in that fight.

Advertising agencies come in many shapes and sizes, often not apparent to the uninitiated. Half create the advertising and the other half find the audiences. Some create advertising designed to influence how people *think*, usually in the long term, others create advertising designed to influence what people *do*, usually in the short term. Some claim to do both. Some call themselves 'digital' agencies, but it's a strange distinction because now everything is digital. They are all in the business of ideas.

Channels are sustained by advertising revenue, but often do not think of themselves as being in the advertising industry. The extent to which any business is in the advertising industry is best understood by following the chain of money that delivers their revenue. If the bulk of it comes from advertising, then they are working in the advertising industry. That is going to be quite easy to see for a poster contractor – the sole purpose of the organisation is to erect and manage spaces where advertising can be displayed. It is a little harder to see for newspapers and magazines. Or TV studios. Or Google. Or podcasts. These are all the advertising industry. Without advertising, all these businesses would struggle to get a revenue stream to sustain their profits. Knowing about how advertising works is critical to running these businesses well.

A proliferation of new channels has made advertising much more interesting and much more complicated in recent years. Since the advent of commercial TV in the US in the 1930s, the possible range of types of advertising was largely stable. You could have moving pictures with sound, just sound, just still pictures, just words and no pictures, in big spaces or small spaces. And that was it. TV, cinema, radio, print, posters and classified ads. Then the internet arrived, and everything became a lot more unstable and a good deal more complicated. New formats, new options, rapidly growing or shrinking audiences, and constantly disputed data. It took a little while for everyone to work out their place and then stability began to return. The channels drove this change in the industry and will continue to be the biggest influence because of their impact on audiences.

The arrival of internet-mediated channels is the greatest shift the industry has seen. The power was previously with advertisers. They aggregated multi-million-dollar budgets so they could call the shots. Channels that carried advertising had to court them to get their money. The advertisers mastered the channels very quickly and discussion about how best to create, say, a TV ad, happened between clients and agencies. TV stations rarely ever got involved, sticking instead to working out how to make great TV shows.

The rise of Google and Facebook has changed this fundamentally. It is important to note that the rise of the internet did not make this inevitable. Prior to the arrival of these companies, the internet wasn't a great advertising channel, and could have developed as a home of subscription services and paid-for software, rather than the ad-funded free-to-use model that now predominates. The internet facilitated the growth of Google and Facebook, but the rules of digital advertising have been written by two commercial companies who decided how to make it work. They now have more power than any of the advertisers on their channels, they dictate best practice, changing formats and standards in their favour with little need to consult anyone else. For now, they are the rulers of the industry.

**Key ideas:**

Despite an ever-growing number of players in the advertising business and the blurring of lines between them all, at its heart are two distinct activities: creating messages and finding audiences for those messages.

*Now let's take a more detailed look at each of these players, starting with the agencies.*

# Chapter 3

# Agencies – the ideas people

The first known advertising agent in the world was William Taylor, who advertised himself as such in London in 1786. The services he offered were those of an intermediary between those with products or services to promote and media channels that needed the funding advertising could provide. He would take a brief, write the adverts (most advertisements at the time featured only text), negotiate a price with the media owner and take a little to pay himself along the way. Nowadays we tend to think of advertising agencies as a branch of the 'creative industries', but the origin story of the agency is a reminder that their core function is more commercial than creative. There was little glamour associated with the transaction. But over time, things changed.

A whole range of services began to be added to this core function. Pictures were added to the words, along with strategic thinking, research and business analysis. Media strategy was added to advise on an increasing range of channel options. This became the 'full-service' agency with teams of specialists marshalled by a business director.

Over time, as each of these services became more sophisticated, those who ran advertising agencies realised that money could be made by separating the core functions of an agency into entirely different companies. Media planning and buying was spun off, and globe-straddling media agencies appeared. Each advertising specialism was housed in a different company, owned by a holding company that could offer clients a wide range of marketing services, including design, branding, advertising, direct response and much more. The world's largest advertising agency is London's WPP, who describe themselves like this:

> '*WPP is a creative transformation company. We build better futures for our people, clients and communities.*'

Their main competitor, and the second biggest in the world, Omnicom, has this to offer:

> '*Omnicom is an inter-connected global network of leading marketing communications companies.*'

There is little doubt that William Taylor would struggle to recognise himself here. Advertising agencies no longer describe themselves using either of the words 'advertising' or 'agency'. This tells us something about the industry's desired self-image in an age of considerable technological disruption. Advertising alone is not enough.

## Agency roles

Aside from the functions common to any business (finance, and human resources) the three core departments in any agency are client management (usually called 'account handling'), strategy (sometimes called 'planning') and creative (which includes production). Each function has a very specific role and character – the differences between disciplines in any one agency are often greater than the differences between the same discipline across different agencies.

## Client management

Client management is how an agency makes money (or fails to do so). Account handlers in agencies have job descriptions that combine diverse skills. They need the creative judgement associated with the agency's core product, and the business acumen to ensure that the agency is profitable. They determine how the agency gets paid, define the size and skills of the team needed to serve the client and run the processes that deliver the creative product. Some account handlers see their job as mainly about client entertaining, ensuring the clients are happy and their every whim catered for. Others see their job as leading the client to a brilliant creative outcome (with positive results both for the brand and for the agency's reputation). Most try to find a balance between these extremes.

The most effective account handlers are tireless polymath raconteurs, able to do a little bit of everyone else's role, if required. Those who become agency CEOs were most often account handlers in their early years.

## Strategy

Strategy was the last standalone discipline to emerge in advertising agencies but has proven tremendously valuable to clients and lucrative to agencies. The agency strategy function makes a connection between business analysis and creativity.

Agency strategists share some DNA with management consultants; nowhere near the same degree of data-driven rigour but with more flair for lateral thinking. Many see their responsibility to the brand they are working with, or the quality of the creative product that results, rather than to the agency's business success. This instinctive dedication to impartiality often makes the strategist the clients' favourite person on the agency team, the one to whom they turn to for unbiased counsel.

Their job is to take as much information as they can get in the time available, about the business, audience, competitors and broader culture, then turn that into a brand strategy. A brand strategy will determine the type of advertising that is made, the emotions it seeks to evoke or the specific benefits it should communicate, and to whom. It is a poetic expression of business and market analysis. Strategists turn information and data into simple stories of potential transformation communicated in presentations to the clients and briefing documents for the creative teams.

The skills of a strategists are sometimes referred to as being 'T-shaped' – they need a breadth of reference points to understand the culture that brands operate in, teamed with a depth of knowledge about the specific product, service, or industry at hand. Some strategists are much more interested in broad concepts and business dynamics, others much more engaged by tweaking the executions that emerge.

In media agencies the process is similar, although the output is a media plan that defines the channels that give the best return for the client's budget.

## Creative

As creative work is usually the main thing that most clients are paying an advertising agency to do, creative is the only totally indispensable function. The people in agency creative departments are usually referred to simply as 'creatives' as though they have a monopoly on creativity and creative thinking. Their job is to come up with the ideas. As a result, they are given a peculiar amount of power, with the head of the creative department often the only person in an agency with absolute power of veto on the output of their department. It is the very best job in the world and the very worst job in the world. Creatives are paid (often very handsomely) to come up with creative ideas, all day long. But most of their ideas get rejected, by their boss, their colleagues, the clients or the research company.

The behaviour and character of creative teams is highly variable. Some are collaborative and consensual, interested in working as part of a team and keen to involve other disciplines and the client too. Others are much more isolationist, hostile and adversarial, challenging other departments and the client to bring them the very best opportunities, which they work on with their door closed, and invite few others in to help. However they behave, their motivations are firstly to get their ideas out into the world (which can be a surprisingly hard job), and secondly to win awards for those ideas. Awards shape the careers of creative people, the path to higher salaries and more responsibility. This striving for award-winning work is important when seeking to understand the culture and operation of any advertising agency. Ideas are judged not only for their potential to build a client's business, but also for their ability to enhance the agency's reputation.

The creative department, in larger agencies at least, is then supplemented by production resources that help to bring ideas to life, from design, through TV production and photography. This then stretches out in an ecosystem of independent production companies, contracted to make the adverts themselves.

## Different types of agency

There are three main types of agency, which all have different balances of the functions described above (it could be argued that now there are four, with the rise of the digital agency, but more of that later). The creative agency is the ad agency of popular imagination and set the structure that ultimately gave birth to the other types of agency as time went on, so it is a good place to start.

## The creative agency

Creative agencies exist to make ads. They are often not called 'ads', for fear of seeming old fashioned, but for clarity we will stick with that terminology. Their thinking is not abstract, but tangible, always pushing towards getting something made. Many of them will claim to have a unique process to do this, often expressed in an intricate diagram of boxes and arrows, perhaps in the shape of a butterfly. But in reality, the process is broadly the same in every agency. The client usually instigates things, having written a brief that will describe the tasks they are looking for the agency to put their mind to. It will define the brand, product or service, audience and budget. It may raise tricky strategic or creative questions for the agency to solve.

Sometimes it specifies the channels they want to use, sometimes they will brief the media agency to answer that question.

At this point the work of the creative agency begins. The strategy function starts to apply their minds to the brief (although in smaller agencies, the client brief will go straight to the creatives). Whoever does it, there is always an initial stage of working out what the message should be, turning the clients' objectives into a set of words that will inspire creativity. The strategy and planning function is considering what is likely to work to produce the desired outcome, whether sales or behaviour. This might be a rational message (a fact to associate with the brand), a more abstract concept (a new way to think about the role of the brand in your life), or an emotion (how they want the brand to feel). Strategists will usually have strong views about what will and will not work. These are informed by more or less data, depending on the approach of the individual strategist, the sensibilities of the agency they work in or the type of brief they are dealing with.

If the brief is for Pepsi, for example, this might initially look rather simple: after all it is just a drink, in one flavour, with sugar or not. But the choices in messaging are much broader than that. Should Pepsi be positioned as the alternative to Coca Cola, using tests to prove it tastes better (the '*Pepsi Challenge*')? Or should the focus be on refreshment and product appeal, making people want to drink it there and then? Or perhaps Pepsi should associate itself with the passions of a new generation of drinkers, whose parents chose Coca Cola ('*The Choice of a New Generation*')? Or maybe the investment should instead be made in sponsoring global sporting vents and entertainment properties, and advertising that connection? Even with a very simple product, the strategic choices are wide, and each would lead to very different advertising.

Strategists are also thinking about what will inspire the best creative work. Rarely is the agency's strategic output ever seen by anyone other than the client and agency itself, so it is only worth doing if it changes the direction of creative work, versus what the creatives would have done had they simply worked directly to the client's brief. The best strategists balance their obligations to effectiveness and creativity beautifully and see no contradiction between them.

Once the brief is agreed, usually after a check-in with the client, then creatives get to work. This creative process has two distinct phases, each requiring different ways of thinking. The first is the search for ideas. It does not respect office hours and is somewhat hard to control. Ideas will appear unbidden in the middle of the night, when the brain is resting, making connections between the specific problem outlined in the brief (the details of the product, brand, audience, channels, etc.) and their general exposure to culture (movies, TV shows, other ads, your Facebook feed, etc.). This process was described and codified in 1940 by James Webb Young, in his book *A Technique for Producing Ideas.* His thesis was that interesting ideas happen when you connect something of direct relevance to the brief you are working on with something that comes from your store of general knowledge about the world. For anyone who has ever worked in advertising, this makes immediate intuitive sense. To illustrate with a famous recent example, the Dove Campaign for Real Beauty comes from an understanding of the effect of Dove beauty products on a range of skin types and body shapes with an insight into how women feel about the debate on over-idealised representation of women in popular culture.

The inspiration is only half the story. The next phase is turning this idea into executions that can do it justice. In the past, this was often a single piece of creative work that could reach most of a desired audience. A poster, print or TV ad that would be shown repeatedly and the message communicated. Nowadays things are a good deal more complex, as even modest and low-budget campaigns will require multiple executions before you can be confident that most of your audience have been exposed to the idea. Whether they are ads on Facebook, six-second YouTube bumpers, posters, TV ads, or one of the many other options available, each needs to be thought through and structured before presentation. Then it is common for a lot of this work done by creative teams to be dismissed by the creative director and then they have to start again, before the client sees anything. It is a tough process.

Once everyone is happy, the client gets to see the work. This initial contact can sometimes be called a 'tissue meeting', for reasons that few understand (is it because the ideas at this stage were once scribbled on disposable paper? Nobody seems to know for sure), but the important thing is that ideas are lightly worn and disposable at this point. Client and agency enter this conversation panning for gold, but usually aware that it may not be immediately visible to the naked eye. Even in the age of Big Data, this process is usually based entirely on intuition. Some research might be imminent, but it is usually qualitative and the process of choosing what gets tested is down to the taste and whims of the agency and the client. This might be considered the triumph of humanity in an age of machines, or an infuriatingly subjective and wasteful process when messages can now easily be tested online in real time. Brand-building through advertising is an inexact science, and whilst there is always data available, nothing is totally predictive of real-world outcomes.

The agency is responsible for managing the journey from brief through ideas to execution. Whether big or small budgets, multi-channel or single execution, there is always a decision-making process where the agency tries to protect and advocate its work before getting to production. There is an accommodation sought between what the creatives had in mind and the client's view of their work. The best agencies and clients use this process to make the output much better.

Through the process of discussions and research a decision gets made and then some work is produced. This usually happens through third-party production companies, film-makers, animators, photographers, illustrators, in a process managed by the agency. Once these things have been made, they are then deployed in the market by a media agency, who have been going through their own process to get to this point.

## The media agency

In recent history, media was a department of every ad agency. There would be a media planner on each team and their responsibility would be to ensure that the work reached an audience. The media function in advertising is split into two broad areas, media strategy and media buying; very different activities, skill sets and people, both vital to delivering the right result to the client and brand.

Media agencies deal with the much less discussed, but in some ways much more important, side of advertising. Devising a message and then making creative execution looks much more exciting and interesting, but the core issue for most advertisers is how to find an engaged audience. Exceptional creative can build its own audience by being shared online (particularly if those doing the sharing are famous and popular enough to lead millions of others to their content). Many campaigns that win creative awards will claim this effect, even quantifying the 'value' of this audience exposure when calculating return on invest-ment. But the number of advertisements that benefit in this way is a vanishingly small percentage of everything that is made. It is a gamble, not a strategy. Media agencies do something different and more valuable.

If you find yourself in a media agency, you will initially see few differences to the world of the creative agency. The central location, posh coffee and designer furniture all look quite similar, but there is a subtle difference in the people and a big difference in what they are doing. Media agency folk often consider themselves more accountable and closer to business realities than creative agency staff. Their currency is more about maths than ideas, but their self-image is conflicted as they find themselves at the intersection of two very powerful current forces in business.

They are in the advertising industry, so they are ideas companies. They can be a bit miffed that some refer to their executional counterparts as 'creative agencies', because being 'creative' is something we all admire and want to be. And in business it often comes with an intangible value that enables zeroes to be added to the end of a fee proposal. As a result, their media strategies will claim to be 'idea-driven' and many media agencies will have invested in hiring creative teams from ad agencies.

But increasingly, they are also in the tech industry, so they are data companies. Everything they do is data driven and they spend a lot of time with Google and Facebook to reassure the client that they are in the new economy, delivering predictable and defined outcomes, to be efficient and eliminate wastage by adapting the message to the audience. If there is one thing that clients want more than creativity, it is evidence that they are using data in their business. It does not take much reassurance about data to boost a stock price, or to depress the stock price of your competitors. Media agencies want and need to be part of this world. The primacy of data could enable them to become the client's closest partner, as automation threatens to eat away at the role of the creative agency.

Much as in the creative agency, everything starts with the client brief for the media agency. The brief will ask the media agency to do one of two things – either to use a defined budget in the most effective way possible, or to define a budget to achieve a task. Marketing budgets are often based on how much a company feels they can spare, or how much they spent the previous year. It is unusual for a budget to be entirely determined by the task as that would cause havoc in the client's budget-setting process, which usually happens some time before any conversations take place with any agency.

Once the media agency has the budget, the first part of the process is to define an audience. The most potent and emotional concept in audience definition is that of 'wastage', the idea that 'half of my advertising budget is wasted, I just don't know which half' (attributed to John Wanamaker in the US, or Lord Leverhulme in the UK). It sounds sensible and reasonable but is hotly contested by much of the latest research. Wanamaker or Leverhulme believed that paying to show advertising to lots of people who are not in the market was a waste of money. Every dollar put against someone who is not going to buy is a 'waste', and waste must be eliminated in the interests of efficiency. There are (at least) three big problems with this concept. The first is the idea that advertising needs to have an effect right now and return on investment is best measured over days, weeks or months, rather than years. Industry data consistently shows that the biggest effects of advertising are in the long term, so even if someone is not in the market today, their exposure to advertising isn't a waste (because even if they cannot remember having seen it, the impression it creates of the brand will linger). The second is the problem that the more tightly defined an audience is, the higher the cost of reaching them. On a cost-per-person basis, targeted plans cost more than mass-market plans. So, every dollar spent is only going to those in the market, but it costs much more to show each of them your message. The total budget might be less, but only because in the endeavour to cut out 'waste' far fewer people have been reached, reducing the scale of any potential effect on the business. Efficiency at the expense of effectiveness.

There is now a strong (and data-driven) view that all targeting is bunk and the only thing that matters is mass awareness. Advocated by Byron Sharp and the Ehrenberg Bass institute, this work has shaped the thinking of advertisers across the world. Their data shows that the most famous brands in any market tend to get the most sales, and that this fame is measured amongst the entire population, not a niche defined audience. Even if you have never taken part in any athletic endeavour, Nike is probably the first sportswear brand you can name. People without dogs and cats know about Pedigree and Whiskas. These opinions matter, as they tend to correlate very closely with success for these brands, so reaching people out of the market is not a waste after all.

The media planner is weighing all this up when looking at a client's plan. It is a service industry, of course, just like the creative side of the business, so despite being data informed, the plans will always be weighing up a sense of what they think will make the client happy as much as what will deliver the results. The channel choices before them will all have subjective weightings. Some clients think posters do not work. Other clients think TV ads are an extravagance. Most clients think you need Facebook and Google, because that is the modern thing to do (although some will occasionally boycott these channels for fear of getting embroiled in the latest controversy they may have created).

In most cases (aside from the extreme disciples of mass reach) an audience will be defined. This is usually a mixture of demographics (age, gender, location, income, profession, family status) and relationship to the brand and category (preferred brand, frequency of usage). Prior to the arrival of Facebook and Google the next trick was whether media could actually be brought against this target audience and what that really meant. The client brief may define with intricate precision an audience of occasional buyers who have complex feelings about the category. This might be useful for defining the message but useless to the media planner as the channels they want to buy do not 'sell' that audience. And on top of that it is important to remember that all this is survey data. People who at one point said they had those attitudes and happen to have a certain pattern of media consumption. You are buying the probability of a defined audience, at best.

Google and Facebook disrupted this survey-based targeting with something that looked a lot like real people, in real time. Because all their users are individuals, whose behaviour they can track and record, they can offer a target that feels much more precise, because it is based either on interest (the things they seem to look at on Facebook) or intent (the things they search for in Google). Whilst there is plenty of data to vouch for the effectiveness of all the other channels, this story about efficiency has been very compelling for clients and as a result Facebook and Google hoovered up vast swathes of the global advertising market (in tandem, of course, with hoovering up a vast amount of the time and attention of the global population).

As these new channels have appeared, very few old channels have disappeared, so the job of the media planner is to create and build the most efficient jigsaw of reach for the defined audience. If the defined audience is 20 to 30-year-old Facebook users, then the job is simpler than trying to target a wide range of the population. There are of course plenty of them who no longer watch broadcast TV, and live a life mediated through their smartphones. But there are also plenty who do not own a smartphone and watch lots of commercial TV. Posters are great if the audience is urban, but not much use in rural areas with few advertising sites. And so on. The media planner needs to fill in as many of these gaps as is sensible and efficient. The final plan will usually be expressed as a combination of reach (what percentage of the defined audience are likely to see the advertising) and frequency (how many times will they see any of the adverts in the campaign). This is communicated in phrases like '80% at 2+', or if it is a TV plan, then maybe they will talk about '300 ratings'. This number is arrived at by multiplying the percentage coverage of the audience by the frequency, so with 300 ratings, it is 100% of the audience seeing the ad three times, on average. The bigger the number, the more confidence there is that the message will get through to the right audience.

Everything after that (even with Google and Facebook) is a matter of faith. The best that can be guaranteed is that the audience are somewhere near your advert when it appears (they have bought a copy of the magazine, but nobody can know if they looked at any given page). Even Google and Facebook, who do know more than most about whether things have been seen, are surprisingly evasive on the matter. It is tough to get to the bottom of this. Good media planners and effective marketing people usually just take things on faith that if they have enough messaging out there, near enough to the audience, then good things will probably happen for the brand.

There is a further consideration for the media planner in the choice of channels, as they are far from equal in their effects and potential. Production costs and impact on the audience will vary dramatically. Even the most rudimentary TV ads will cost tens of thousands of dollars to make, whereas a simple display ad online (or a text ad on Google) is almost free to produce. This is why many clients will say that TV advertising is 'expensive', whereas what they probably mean is that TV advertising requires a more substantial upfront investment, which is not a great use of money if the audience is small, or if they have very little capital to spend on the media budget. The only sensible way to think about cost is with a cost-per-contact method, dividing any upfront costs across the entire audience. For big brands, those more 'expensive' channels then start to look rather low cost indeed. The impact on the audience is the other main consideration, with TV advertising (and video more generally) continually proven to be the most effective way to get a message across and plant a memory in the mind of the audience. The medium can also be the message, with big budget TV ads demonstrating the power and prestige of a brand.

There are further considerations for media planners that may have been covered in the client brief. The main factor is how quickly the client is hoping for a return on their investment. If they want to get a direct response, with potential customers clicking to purchase (or in the old days, calling up a phone number), then they will look for channels that can deliver response quickly at relatively low cost. Channels that help drive action. These are often information heavy, like print, or very close to point of purchase, like online banners. However, if they are looking for the advertising to build their brand to deliver long-term results over time, then other types of channel will come in to play, channels that help create memory (of the brand, not of the ads). These are often involving and emotional, like TV or cinema.

Partnerships and sponsorships offer the media agency much more scope for creativity, perhaps cutting out the creative agency altogether. An interesting connection between a brand and a media owner can be a creative statement in its own right. TV stations, newspapers, magazines, radio stations and even poster contractors now all have creative departments of sorts, who can offer creative execution as well as media space. And many media agencies now also have their own creative departments who can generate ideas for such partnerships and put them in place.

As with many things in the modern advertising industry, the growth of Google and Facebook, along with other digital advertising providers, has complicated matters somewhat. A good deal of their success has been in cutting agencies out of the process of planning and buying advertising entirely. They enable businesses of all sizes to reach big audiences with sophisticated messaging on a self-serve basis. They also have advertising products that combine many of the benefits of more traditional channels. The power of video can be accessed via YouTube or Facebook or Instagram without needing to use TV. Just text and image can be used too, but with the benefit of being able to test multiple variations of image and headline and see what works best. This has presented both a threat and an opportunity for media agencies. With so many more choices available (often with less well-established effectiveness track records), the need for expert advice in how to spend media money is greater than ever. The business success of Facebook and Google makes them interesting and powerful partners for clients who are keen to access them direct, and there is a generation of start-ups who cannot see why they would need a media agency at all, as they can do it all in-house at much lower cost.

## The direct agency

Some would question whether direct agencies should be a part of a book about advertising at all. What they do is perhaps closer to sales than advertising, by some definitions, but if you ask people on the receiving end, then of course it is advertising. As we mentioned earlier, many direct agencies would probably call themselves ideas companies, like everyone does, for all the same reasons we outlined earlier.

There is a little less to say about the direct agency, as we have covered the process in the previous two sections and it is similar for the direct agency, often working with a media agency as ad agencies do. So, let us look at what is different.

There is certainly a different character to direct agencies, as they do a different job. If advertising agencies are dedicated to building memories about brands, then direct agencies are creating immediate action. They want clicks, calls or visits right away. Whilst much of the value generated by the ad agency is felt over months or years, the value created by the direct agency might be measured in minutes or hours. The discipline is quite different, because action works differently to memory. Ad agencies employ simplifiers, who boil brands down to their essence to plant simple associations. Direct agencies are full of people dedicated to telling as much as they can to compel people to do something. It is still an art, a craft, but a very different one.

The people and the roles are superficially similar (business-people, strategy people and creative people), but the direct agency deals more in maths than poetry. They aim to deliver low cost per response, by targeting exactly the right people with the right message. When it comes to advertising, it can be argued that it doesn't really matter whether the audience are imminently in the market for what's being sold. When it comes to direct, it really does matter.

Direct agencies will always start with the data, crunching numbers to work out who their audience are and where they are. In the past, the bulk of the work was in direct mail – buying and using lists of addresses and sending them paper through the post. That is still a big part of the role, but a large part of the business has shifted online, with pixels now as important as paper. Direct agencies control costs and focus on returns. They are much less concerned with aesthetics, designing more for effect than appearance. They will create many variants of messaging and be constantly testing to discover which works best, whereas the ad agency is constantly trying to create a singular statement about the brand to bring everyone towards it, aggregating the audience around the message. The direct agency segments, cutting the audience in the most economically efficient slivers, each with a precision targeted message. There is surprisingly little crossover of people between direct and ad agencies. What looks almost the same from the outside is very different on the inside. Both the skills required and the philosophical approach are so different that they rarely ever switch disciplines.

Everyone in a direct agency is generally much closer to how their communication works, able to apply the 'rules' of direct marketing. Creativity in a direct agency can often be more in the use of data or the identification of an audience or opportunity that others might have missed (although there is still considerable craft in the writing of words that drive action). The strategy and data functions are more numerous and more important. Creative people in direct agencies are generally more flexible and collegiate than their opinionated counterparts in ad agencies. This is partly because they are constantly creating variants for testing, rather than putting all their conviction behind a single idea.

The divide between advertising and direct marketing seems to be based on two entirely different views about how advertising works and what it is for. Does it work on the subconscious, creating memories that deliver associations with brands in the long term, ensuring that they are preferred at the moment of choice? Or does it work with the rational brain, driving action in the here and now, easily measurable and able to be optimised? Both roles are important and complementary. Brands with positive associations generally deliver better return on investment from their direct activity. The optimal marketing plan often involves the services of both ad agencies and direct agencies, working together. Brand advertising is often more effective with bigger and more established brands. More direct activity helps to provide the momentum needed by smaller businesses that are just setting out, their investors less patient for the effects of brand advertising. A certain critical mass of distribution and potential customers is needed to make mass advertising really pay back.

Direct agencies are often teamed with performance marketing teams in media agencies, where in contrast with the creative side, direct response work is more usually a department rather than a different type of media agency. The direct agency has some advantages over the traditional ad agency, with access to data and a sensibility that is better suited to a world where the internet dominates media choices.

The challenge faced by direct agencies in recent years is the legal restriction on use of data. One of the main avenues for reaching people was the use of lists of names, addresses, phone numbers. But in the wake of increasing concern about privacy and the use of such data, GDPR (General Data Protection Regulation) laws came in across Europe to effectively outlaw the targeting of anyone who had not given their explicit permission to receive marketing materials. Legal restrictions on the use of personal data are only likely to increase, making the job of the direct agency tougher.

## The holding companies

Before we leave the world of the agencies, we should briefly discuss holding companies. Initially, advertising agencies were domestic affairs, growing through working with more and more clients, but in most markets, there's a limit to how many clients any agency can have, as most are not happy about agencies working with their competitors. So, the bigger agencies in the US, France, UK and Japan sought international expansion, acquiring agencies in other countries, or setting up local offices under a global brand name. This coincided with the globalisation of clients who would then often align their business with the same agency band name across the world. Models of service varied, sometimes a very centralised operation with a global hub in New York, Paris, London or Tokyo creating work that was then distributed across the world; sometimes a loosely connected set of local operations united by a similar communications idea or set of design and identity principles. These global networks developed before the separation of media and creative agencies, as that happened, global media networks appeared in parallel. But of course, there are only so many countries in the world to expand to, and only so many global clients. Agency growth came through separate companies acquiring a number of different agency brands and operating them as a single entity. The separation of the agency brands within the holding company enables them to handle competing brands from the same market, removing that impediment to growth. WPP and Omnicom are the biggest holding companies at present, owning agencies that work in a dizzying array of disciplines. The holding company sometimes deals directly with clients, to co-ordinate teams of agencies, and cut global deals on fees. They also operate co-ordinated media buying functions, where their clout pays off for clients. On the creative side there are some benefits to be gained from scale (more talented management teams can spread their skills across a broader range of clients), but in what remains a handmade creative business this advantage can be overstated.

**Key ideas:**

> Whilst there are some economies of scale to be had, and advantages in a global network, the agency world remains a cottage industry, relying on the talents of individuals with no one company ever achieving dominant market share. Each type of agency might look similar from the outside, but they have very different cultures and activities.

*Perhaps the more influential part of the advertising industry is the role of the client.*

# Chapter 4

# Clients – the marketing people

Most advertising is paid for by marketing departments. Small businesses sometimes make advertising the responsibility of the CEO or a founding entrepreneur, but it is generally the marketing department. Advertising is one of a broader range of marketing responsibilities. These are well defined by Jerome McCarthy's four Ps of 1960's marketing theory: Product (what is being sold and how can it be improved?), Price (how much should be charged?), Place (where will it be sold?) and Promotion (the advertising bit – how will people discover it?).

Clients who work in companies where marketing is marginalised may find themselves only doing one of the Ps: Promotion. Advertising can be seen as a flaky and questionable use of people's time and the organisation's scarce resources. Marketing can be dismissed as the 'colouring-in department', whilst the real grown-ups get on with the business of counting the money. Media spend is something to be minimised or indulged in every so often. Effects are often expected to appear very quickly, and when they do not, the whole endeavour is dismissed as failure. The fact that this goes against most of the empirical evidence about how advertising works is not well understood.

By contrast, clients who work in companies where marketing is central will find themselves involved in a wide range of decisions, usually backed by customer data, and have stable and consistent marketing budgets to work with. Marketing investment is seen as a way to build and improve the business, a growth engine, not a cost to cut. In many tech companies, advertising investment is such a core function that it drives the stock price and is of pressing interest to the CEO and board. Without physical retail presence, advertising operates as a storefront for these companies. Without it, they would have no business at all. In the tech economy companies with very low advertising budgets can be seen by investors as lacking ambition and find it hard to attract the kind of investment needed to keep them going.

For the client, dealing with the advertising agency is near the end of the process, not the beginning. The much bigger part of the job is in finding, justifying and protecting budgets. Agencies spend most of their time thinking about ideas and audiences. Most clients do not have that luxury. A surprisingly large amount of their time is spent turned inward, presenting to colleagues and asking for more money (or asking to hold on to the money they have). Their primary role is to use shareholders' money effectively, to build a marketing team, train them and codify the knowledge your company has gained over the years about how to do marketing well. They participate in cross-functional company-wide initiatives to create a sense of shared purpose between departments, they sit with finance going over the numbers again, they take part in myriad other activities that distract from the thing that the ad agency really thinks they should mainly be doing: working with them.

Agencies can fail to understand clients in a number of important ways. Agencies assume clients want explosive growth, whereas steady and predictable sales are almost always preferable (agencies love the short-term drama of hockey stick growth curves; clients fret about capacity in the factory and the performance that might be expected in the following year). Agencies are often disdainful of 'rules' whereas clients know that embedding best practice helps them avoid problems. Agencies do not much like research, particularly quantitative 'pre-testing' of advertising, but clients need to justify the investments they make to many internal stakeholders. Agencies pursue novelty and like to change things as much as possible to keep things interesting, good clients know that consistency is the way that brands are best built.

## Different types of client company.

Marketing plays very different roles in different industries, with advertising playing either a starring or supporting role in turn. The dynamics are very different, and worth knowing when considering how advertising works.

## FMCG (fast moving consumer goods) companies

The discipline of brand management was created and codified by Neil McElroy at Procter & Gamble in an internal memo in 1931. This suggested that each brand should be run as a small business, organised around the brand, not organised around the other departments of the company. The success of P&G in subsequent years led this template to be widely adopted across the entire consumer goods marketing industry. FMCG companies like P&G, Unilever and SC Johnson, make products that are frequently purchased ('fast moving' because they do not sit on supermarket shelves for very long). Advertising plays a big role for these brands, because the decision to buy them or not is taken frequently, and almost always in the presence of all the competitors. The most important thing is getting your product in the store in the first place – the more shelf space, the more sales. This trade marketing is sometimes the job of the sales department and is linked to advertising (more space can be secured in store with the promise to spend a lot of media money on an advertising campaign). For many FMCG companies, the amount they spend to secure this space, often by promising discounts or offers, is greater than the amount they spend on advertising. Innovation is also a big deal, inventing new packaging, new formulations, thinking about what consumers want nowadays and what they might want in the future. A lot of advertising in FMCG is for launches and improvements. The biggest categories are food and household items (detergents, shampoo, etc.), often from companies with a long heritage, and very well-developed marketing cultures. They have depth of experience, understand the power of marketing and have codified it in ways of working. They are also often multi-national, enabling each country to learn from another and moving their people around the world, bringing the best people to the biggest brands, irrespective of nationality. Whilst this model faces significant challenge from the changes delivered by the internet (more of which later), it still works, and the bulk of their sales comes through physical stores, rather than online (although almost all are now also exploring a direct sales model to complement it).

## Automotive

The automotive industry has driven the history and practice of advertising almost as much as FMCG. Car brands like Ford, BMW and Nissan have been at the centre of economies (particularly the US, Germany and Japan) and have used advertising to create desirable brands that matter more than the facts of their engineering. These companies became ambassadors for the countries themselves, the brands embodying national traits (American freedom, German efficiency, Japanese precision). Cars should be the most rational of all purchases (given quite how much money is at stake) but over the years advertising has made it anything but rational.

In recent years, two factors have totally changed what it means to create advertising in this industry – globalisation and the internet. As products became standardised across the world, marketing and advertising became ever more centralised for most car companies. In the past, model specifications, designs, names and launch dates would differ by country, and certainly by region, meaning lots of local advertising, controlled in the local market and adapted for the local culture. As that has changed, so has the dynamic of the industry. Car advertising is now created regionally or globally, breaking the link between the advertising and in-market performance. In a traditional model, those creating the advertising would have their hands on all the levers and the effect would be felt in sales and brand measures. In the globalised model, the audience becomes primarily internal, with the core metric being the number of markets that choose to run the work and the amount of media money they spend behind it. Once that sell-in process is done, then the global team moves on to the next task. In a sense, the car industry has always worked a little like this, due to the role of the dealers. Automotive brands are effectively a business-to-business operation, with the car companies selling to the dealers and then the dealers selling to the drivers. The advertising is just part of the package that convinces the dealers to make orders. In many ways, it is more important that the dealers like the advertising than whether or not the potential drivers are persuaded by the advertising.

Over time, it is forecast that most of the car industry will become products people share, rather than own, changing the dynamics of advertising in this category entirely (perhaps causing it to behave more like contract subscription services).

## Retail

In most countries, retailers like Wal-Mart, Target, Carrefour and Tesco are amongst the biggest advertising spenders. The most prolific retail advertisers are usually supermarkets and most of the advertising they do is about products and prices, with weekly offers designed to attract customers in store. Data suggests that such promotional activity generates very little profitable return for the business (any benefit from the advertising is offset by the cost of discounting the products), but few retailers want to be the first one to pull out, in fear that their competitors will steal all their customers. This fear is often most strongly felt by store managers, who have power in retail organisations and are hard to persuade, as they seek short-term effects above long-term brand preference. Retail advertising is best understood as part of a dance of power between the retailers and the brands they sell. Nowadays, the retailers are usually more powerful, as so many brands are seen as entirely substitutable, whereas store choice can make a big difference to the total price paid for weekly groceries. Retail marketing teams generally spend very little time pondering their marketing model or redefining their brand diamond, onion, pyramid, or whatever other diagrammatic metaphor they favour. They are instead too busy getting the advertising out in the market and getting the customers in. Retail marketing is the home of activists, not philosophers. It is also intensely local. Most retail brands are either national brands, or nationally managed brands, very tightly linked to physical space. The main driver of success in retail is the number of stores, so advertising plays a secondary role, supporting the visibility of high street storefronts. Opening and fitting out new stores is so important in retail that the marketing department has little or nothing to do with it. Their job is to use communication outside stores to get people into the stores.

## Telecoms, finance and utilities (subscription services)

Telecoms and financial services account for another big chunk of global advertising spend. They are very different categories, but the important characteristic they share is that they are trying to get people to commit to annual contracts. In retail, your customers wander past your store and can enter someone else's store anytime they like. That is not how it works when a customer has signed up to an annual contract for their car insurance or their smartphone. Marketing in this category is all about keeping existing customers and attracting new ones (in the UK, the telecoms company O2 put their rewards programme at the very centre of their advertising, seemingly talking only to their own customers, but actually presenting a picture of what it might be like to be an O2 customer to the entire population). This process is now often mediated by online price comparison sites, which have become amongst the biggest advertising spenders themselves, reducing brand advertising spend in finance in particular, as the smaller players focus spending on these sites rather than going direct to customers.

The marketing job is split between devising loyalty and retention mechanics, and incentives to join, both tangible and intangible. The decisions customers make about whether to join and whether to stay are both emotional and rational – how they feel about the brand and the deal that is being offered. The biggest and most favourably regarded brands will usually have the best retention rates and often charge the highest prices to existing customers. The advertising model is to be in market for as long as possible, so that customers making a decision will be aware of your presence at the right moment. Adspend at any moment during the year could be said to have a lot of 'wastage' in it, but the annual adspend will have virtually none, as everyone's annual contract comes up for renewal at some point. A good deal of the marketing role here is taken up with direct marketing and CRM (customer relationship management) as, unlike in FMCG, the brands have contact details for all their customers and the permission to use them. It is also possible to gather much more direct data about usage of services. This can enable insightful analysis of where customers see the value, and where the costs lie, so products and services can be improved and even personalised.

## Technology

The fastest growing category of spend in recent years has been amongst tech companies, as they are the fastest growing and most profitable companies in the world (although it is not entirely clear whether the advertising is the cause or the effect here). Samsung is now the biggest advertising spender in the world, having overtaken all the FMCG companies that traditionally topped this list. Tech can be a confusing label as it can be used to cover a range of different companies in many categories, including Amazon (the 'everything company' that defies categorisation) Google and Facebook (probably better understood as media and entertainment), Apple and Samsung (mainly smartphones and tablets). Much advertising in this category is driven by the product people, hence the dramatically lit, lingering shots of the devices rotating in space to show them off from every angle, even though most of them look pretty much the same. In the smartphone category, much of this advertising is conducted in partnership with the telecoms networks, with both companies sharing the bill.

Google and Facebook make most of their money from advertising as well as being advertisers themselves. In these innovative tech giants, marketing can be seen as a somewhat frivolous discipline, and advertising only really fully understood as a data-driven, micro-targeted, personally adapted direct response channel. Brand advertising is often more about reputation management than it is about gathering new users.

These companies are near ubiquitous (outside China at least) with universal awareness and constant usage. They advertise the products and services that sit outside their core (like Google's Pixel smartphone), and the rest of their brand work is about making you feel warm towards them as companies (partly to deter governments from legislating against them).

## Media and entertainment

One of the least discussed, but nonetheless very significant sources of advertising spend is the area of media and entertainment. Until recent years, the bulk of this was for content itself, most specifically, movies. The global movie industry has been a huge spender on advertising, producing work that has an entirely different ethos and structure to advertising in other categories. It might seem odd to point it out, but rather than communicating the benefit of the product, showcasing the users, or communicating the price, movies instead offer a sample of the experience, or a striking image. This advertising is either produced in-house, or with a very specialist agency – an industry within the industry. Adjacent to movies is advertising for subscription TV services and the streaming giants Netflix, Amazon Prime and now Disney+. They behave more like subscription services, with half their time spent advertising their price and package to attract new subscribers, and the other half showcasing content. Unlike the movie industry, their content acts as a hook to subscriptions, in a sense they don't really mind how many people watch the advertised show. It just needs to be sufficiently enticing to make customers want to sign up and stay signed up (the bulk of viewing on the streaming platforms is actually taken up by old

TV shows, that are rarely the subject of their splashy advertisements). And then there is the vast array of other media channels that often advertise to attract audiences: news brands, TV channels, radio stations. All are in the business of building audiences but are not advertising to directly achieve business success. Instead, their advertising creates the product they sell, as their revenue comes from selling the presence and attention of these audiences to other advertisers. In all these organisations, those who make the content that is advertised are far more important than those who encourage people to come and see it, so the marketing role can be rather underdeveloped and much less at the heart of that business.

## Charities and government

Advertising for governments and charities is not a huge part of global advertising spend. But it is a huge proportion of the advertising that wins creative awards. This tells us a lot about the culture and priorities of the advertising industry. Charities are mainly concerned with raising funds, although some will also use advertising to campaign on issues as part of their charitable purpose. The fundraising activities are usually unglamorous and rigorously tuned for maximum return. Issue-based communication will not have much media spend behind it, so is often designed to shock, or otherwise attract coverage from news media. In fact, when such advertisements are trying to win awards, they will often promote this coverage as the main 'effect' they have created – advertising as publicity. Clients working for charities need to beware agencies bearing gifts. These agencies are often mainly trying to attract news coverage for themselves by using a charity's brand or cause to create a newsworthy piece of work and win some awards. These ads are often offered to the charity for free but can take up a lot of time and attention and potentially some media spend. A smart charity client can use this to help further their cause, but many charities end up wasting media money on brand communication that never reaches critical mass and is never part of the organisation's total communication strategy.

Government advertising often has a very different set of objectives, usually designed to help change the behaviour of the population. Advertising's role here is to inform people of services the government offers (to help ensure that the people who will benefit are aware of their right to access it, and to make sure the wider electorate sees the government's good works), or to shape people's behaviour to ease their burden on the public purse (typically ensuring they do not injure themselves on the road, or become unhealthy through other poor choices). Behaviour change is an area that has attracted a huge amount of academic attention in recent years, with agencies getting clued up on behavioural economics. Nowadays, agencies seeking government business need to demonstrate how clever they can be in manipulating behaviour indirectly, rather than just delivering a message. There is much greater obligation for government and charity clients to measure the impact of what they have done, often spending much more cash, time and effort on this than their commercial counterparts, as they are spending public money, or that which could otherwise go directly to alleviate suffering. It will also tend to attract some of the most senior and talented agency people, offering interesting topics to apply their brains and creativity to. Having clients in these sectors can be a staff-retention tool for agencies, even though they can deliver very little revenue and usually no profit at all, as everyone spends so much time carefully crafting the work to win those awards. In a sense, charity and government clients act as many agencies' marketing budgets.

## Global or local?

Once almost all advertising was local. But from the eighties onwards, globalisation of the economy began, with brands converging design and packaging principles to enable truly global supply chains and to avoid wasteful cost in designing from scratch in each market. Before long, that logic reached advertising, especially TV. There was incentive on all sides to make this happen, with clients able to spread the costs over many markets and agency creatives able to justify access to vast production budgets for the same reason. The concept of globalisation was enthusiastically popularised by Saatchi & Saatchi, an agency established in London that became global very fast through acquiring other agencies. They then promoted the concept of the global brand, to help create the market they felt they were built to serve. In the late eighties and early nineties, true advertising blockbusters emerged, with a very different character to domestic work. International work has to travel, so tended to favour the role of image and music above dialogue, and abstract spectacle over humour. It was also created in only a few places, connected to the regional or global HQs of the companies commissioning the work – London, Paris, New York, Amsterdam. The inward-looking nature of Japanese culture meant that most Japanese agencies produced work for domestic consumption only and quirks of global distribution often left Sydney and Melbourne producing mainly local work.

Client sectors tend to favour either a local or global approach to advertising. If you work in FMCG, technology, automotive or durables, the advertising will most likely be international (or to put it another way, those working in local roles do not have much control over the advertising). These roles typically involve producing 'assets' that can travel – sets of materials to be adapted to work in local language, using imagery and ideas that work anywhere and do not make much reference to any local culture. A large part of the job is in keeping all the countries onside, so they use the advertising. Advertising roles in retail, telecoms, charities or government are usually local, with the work seeking to make connections and references to local culture. The clients are intimately connected to all parts of the marketing plan and directly accountable for the effect of the work. There are, of course, exceptions, with some global telecoms campaigns and local FMCG brands, but they are unusual.

**Key ideas:**

> Advertising is just one of many responsibilities of a client marketing department, and not always the most important one. Client organisations come in many different shapes and sizes, and understanding the role advertising plays in each sector is vital to produce the kind of advertising they need.

*Where does all this advertising that agencies and clients produce actually appear?*

## Chapter 5

# Channels – where advertising finds audiences

People don't like advertising. They never have. It has been complained about since the 1700s. Some advertising can be entertaining, and some is disliked less than others, but it is all designed to interrupt and distract people from what they would rather be doing. People do love what advertising pays for, especially when they're getting that thing for no or very low cost. Aside from posters on the street, advertising usually accompanies some form of news or entertainment. It has subsidised journalism and popular entertainment (particularly TV) in most countries for many years and is now the favoured funding model for most of the services on the internet. These channels, often referred to collectively as 'media' solve the second question of advertising: how to find an audience. The objective of any channel is in building an audience for advertisers and then measuring that audience in a convincing and stable way. Channels will use this research to either make it easy for clients to buy certain demographics or interests, or to demonstrate the breadth of audiences they will get. This ability to target audiences easily has made both Facebook and Google very compelling options for clients, although questions do still exist about the reliability and quality of the audiences they provide. To understand the choices available to advertisers, we will look at each channel in turn, as the possibilities offered by each differ dramatically. We're not getting into the details of direct marketing or face-to-face sales here and will concern ourselves solely with what most would consider to be advertising media channels, even though they may be used for a range of objectives from brand-building through to direct response.

The role of digital becomes a problem, as far as the terminology goes. When the commercial internet first appeared, a distinction was drawn between analogue and digital channels, which made some sense, for a little while. Now that distinction has become very blurry, as every business uses digital technology both to operate and deliver their services. Many poster sites are now digital rather than paste and paper, many TV channels are watched online rather than on a TV set, radio stations are streamed through smartphones. The internet has come to dominate the advertising industry to such a degree that the next chapter will be entirely devoted to it. Here we will first discuss those channels that have evolved to become digital, having existed in a previously analogue world, where their basic function and dynamics were established, before being enhanced through digital connectivity. Media channels interrupt and distract, and do so either through space or time, sometimes both, drawing primarily either on static visual design or sequential storytelling. Each has advantages and limits that need to be considered, as advertising will need to be adapted for channel, not just in size or form but in the philosophy that is brought to creating the work.

# The different advertising channels

Most channels are paid for on a 'cost per thousand' basis, with simple arithmetic enabling clients to work out how much they are going to pay for each person that might see their adverts. There is then a premium attached to that cost based on the size or length of the ad (bigger and longer costs more, naturally) and the power and desirability of the channel (video tends to be seen to produce a more powerful effect, so often costs more than static image or audio). A smart client and savvy agency will balance these benefits intuitively to produce the best outcome for the money invested.

## Posters

Posters are a version of the oldest, and most clearly understood form of advertising. From sign painting on the walls of ancient archaeological sites, through the bright lights of major cities, to constantly changing digital sites, the poster has endured and adapted, with both great advantages and major drawbacks as a channel. The advantage is that posters are unmissable. Technology and choice allow the avoidance of advertising in most places, but when walking or driving down the street, the posters are just there. People may think they are not looking at them, but much of the evidence suggests that they work their magic on the subconscious brain anyhow. There have been some isolated incidents of cities banning outdoor advertising (Sao Paolo most famously), but it is rare.

The poster is the purest form of advertising. There is a rectangle to play with, of varying orientations and proportions, which people pass at varying speeds depending on location.

Advertisers can choose to fill this rectangle with images, words, just their logo, whatever they like. Some feel that the role of the poster is to get people to look at it (although there are laws against some of the more shocking versions of this, to avoid traffic accidents), but the main role of the poster is to build simple associations around the brand. Some transport sites (bus shelters, rail stations) do enable a lot more, but most posters are at their best with just five words, or a single image plus logo. As the stock of outdoor sites digitises, in common with the rest of the world, all posters begin to work like short-form video, also enabling targeting by time of day and specific location.

## News and magazine brands

Newspapers carried advertising from the very beginning. And for many years, they took the bulk of adspend, largely through individuals or very small businesses using text-only classified advertising. This used to be the role of the front page of the paper, although all this spend has now migrated online and the classified section is no more. They are referred to as news brands here, as it is a bit of a misnomer to call them newspapers as the advertising space they sell is often a hybrid of their print edition and their website. Some, (notably *The Mail* and *The Guardian* from the UK), have a global online audience that dwarfs the circulation of their paper editions. Ads in newspapers tend to exist on a spectrum from mini posters to text-heavy advertorial aping the style of the articles around them. News brands have the advantage of topicality and context, enabling brands to respond to the news, or to produce messaging that they can create at short notice and withdraw within a day (this used to be quite the feature until the internet came along). In many countries, daily newspapers also express political identity, so advertising in them, or not, can make a statement in itself. There is also a lingering degree of prestige to advertising in some news titles, to make a statement about your brand, often at a corporate level. It is the home of offers from the supermarket and open letters from chief execs. Newspapers have suffered as the world has moved online and many now have dwindling circulations and precarious finances. Magazine brands offer something different, often enabling access to audiences with specialist interests (the ever-seductive lack of 'wastage' – if you want to advertise motorcycling gloves, then a motorcycling magazine is probably just the place). There are entire specialist areas of advertising using magazines extensively, with fashion and fragrance dominating the pages of international fashion magazines like *Vogue* and *Elle* that still seem to thrive in print as the rest of the world digitises. Again, the context and prestige of the title is playing a massive role – if this is where the big moves in fashion are made then this is where a fashion or fragrance brand needs to be.

## Radio

Commercial radio has never been glamorous, even though it can offer the best value for money in advertising – big reach, low cost (both media and production). In a visual culture, radio inevitably suffers in image terms, and in the past was perhaps dogged by a feeling that nobody was paying attention. Radio happens in the background, when people are doing something else, and those who own and operate brands do not like to think of themselves as background noise (even though that is what they are, and the data is very clear that it does not matter anyway). It is somehow easier to imagine that people are paying attention to the lavishly crafted TV ad, or the eye-catching poster, and it is certainly much easier to put a picture of these on an office wall, or in an annual report. Radio has also suffered from unintended consequences of advertising regulation. Many categories (finance, telecoms) and types of advertising (limited-time offers) come with terms and conditions attached. That is fine for TV, poster or print, as these terms can run alongside the main visuals, but there is no equivalent in audio, where the terms seem much more alarming, taking up as much prominence as the advertisement itself, and the advertiser pays for every second it takes to read them out. This is not an attractive proposition. But radio remains a very cost-effective and efficient channel. Radio adverts are purely playing with sounds and time, with words and music to deliver the message. There is room for almost limitless creativity on a shoestring budget, although that is not really what most people use radio for, as it tends to be the home of offers and promotions. Nowadays we should really expand the definition of radio to 'audio', as a lot of radio listening happens on the smartphone, via apps. Now Spotify is in many ways the world's biggest commercial radio station, with a revenue model that is a mixture of advertising and subscription income. Much smaller, but still significant for some advertisers (and important to an upscale urban demographic) are podcasts, most of which are exclusively ad supported, with the advertising often woven into the content, as in the early days of radio.

## TV (and cinema)

Since it began in the middle of the last century, TV advertising has become the most powerful advertising media thus created. This role has been challenged recently, as the internet disrupts all media, but the data still supports TV. The power of TV comes not only from extensive reach, but also from the power of video to engage emotions. Yes, making TV advertising can look costly, especially if a brand has a small addressable market, but for big brands with big audiences, profitable returns from TV generally dwarf those of other channels. In common with many other media, TV advertising began by looking like the programmes it interrupted, sometimes embedded within them. But relatively quickly, TV advertising began to develop its own aesthetic of mini dramas, cartoon mascots, celebrity endorsements and product demonstrations. Around the world, the attitude to TV adverts is usually much more positive if your country has not allowed them until recently, or if their supply is relatively restricted. People sometimes even agree that 'the adverts are better than the programmes', which might be a comment on the relative quality of either. When there are many more TV ads, people generally like them less, although whether they liked them at all in the first place is debatable. Advertising of all forms has a parasitic relationship with its context – audiences don't go there for the advertising. TV (and cinema) advertising has a very particular relationship with that context, in that it interrupts something you were probably paying attention to, and makes you wait for the next bit. Radio tends to flow along in the background, so the interruption is much less annoying and other types of advertising tend to disrupt space, rather than time, so they are easy to look away from. This is both TV's power and potentially its ultimate downfall. There is a big appetite for ad-free video, and people are willing to pay for it. It is not a huge factor right now, but if those audiences depart commercially funded TV altogether, then the global advertising industry has a big problem. Audiences can always be reached, but no other media has the power of TV to build brands that endure and grow profits.

The art of the TV ad is in the tense relationship between power and cost, given that you are paying for every second you use (in some markets TV media is sold in 5 or 10 second chunks, and in others by individual seconds). The temptation on the part of those creating the work is to spend longer telling their story, packing in as many messages as possible (the client preference), or slowly building up to the devastating punchline (the creative agency preference). The media agency often plays party pooper, their job being to create the most efficient schedule, and there is always a bit of a tussle over second length. The result is that the archetypal TV ad tends to last for 30 seconds, and most agencies are trained to make best use of this time.

## Sponsorship

Sponsorship is advertising and would be understood as such by most people outside the industry. It is a whole global industry in itself, operating alongside the main ad industry, but it works in a distinctly different way. Whilst most advertising delivers a message through content and creativity, sponsorship seeks to create value for the brand purely through association with something else, usually a sport or entertainment property.

In some ways, it is just about putting the logo in front of an audience and, if chosen carefully, sponsorship can do this very efficiently. Sponsorship deals are usually a good deal more complex than this and brands will often use them to offer access to events for valued customers, or to use as prizes in on-pack giveaways. An element of vanity can be involved, with senior management keen on certain sports or celebrities and justifying the sponsorship investment based largely on this personal enthusiasm. The power of access to the stars of sport and screen is a heady cocktail. Sometimes it works, sometimes not, dependent on how well thought through the association is and how much has been paid for it.

## Events and experiential

Events and experiences feel a lot like advertising but are usually a little closer to sales. There is again an entire adjunct of the advertising industry devoted to this, with even shakier effectiveness models than the main industry. Events can cost a little or an awful lot. Business-to-business marketing (especially where each individual customer has a lot of money to spend) makes big use of events, from participation in conferences and expos to private events. They may be entertaining, or inspirational, simply about perks and relationship-building, or offer free training or otherwise relevant help. Sometimes they are about oiling the wheels of a well-established relationship (although this happens a little less often with new legislation aimed at reducing instances of potential bribery and corruption), or about meeting potential new customers. In the standard consumer world, events are run to offer people a deeper experience of the brand beyond the 30 seconds they see on TV. They are designed to get people involved and will often involve some degree of data capture, either to lead to a sale, or to capture an email address for subsequent marketing. The biggest problem with most experiential work (outside those business-to-business campaigns where customers are few and lucrative) is reach. Compared to almost any form of advertising, the numbers rarely justify the investment. The standard internet-era solution for that problem is to do the event anyway, but then film it and distribute the document of the event online, or make an advert out of it, or a press release. Only 1% of the audience might get involved, but then the other 99% hear about it. This can be a compelling strategy, but only if you planned it that way in the first place. It is otherwise asking a lot of any audience to seek out and enjoy a video of an event that was mainly designed to be experienced in person, in real time.

## Online

There is no way we can do justice to the commercial internet as another media beneath all the other choices listed above. Partly because most of the above media choices are now thoroughly digital, so weave through each of the categories anyhow, and partly because the available choices are so varied and complex. We will look at the impact of online on advertising in the next chapter.

When considering all the options above, advertisers mix channels to achieve their objectives (although it might be surprising how often those objectives are rather vaguely defined, leading to poor choices). A good media schedule combines art and science, based on the simple maths of reach and frequency. To get a message across requires a big enough percentage of the audience exposed to it more than once (this orthodoxy was established when brand management first began as a discipline). Media choices differ most dramatically when there are either big budgets for big audiences, or small budgets for small audiences.

When budgets and audiences are small, the emphasis is generally on response rather than brand-building, so an effect can be measured in the short term and a return on investment established before the money runs out. If a brand-building budget is spent this way, the effect is usually too small to measure, with so few people reached that any change in their views is very hard to measure at a population level. New brands often spend their budget with an emphasis on building trial and usage through direct response, gathering customers as quickly as possible. Nowadays, many of these brands exist primarily or exclusively online, with advertising doing a virtual sales job and the brand itself built through the design of the product or service itself. The intangible value of the brand is built into the experience rather than the advertising.

More established brands will tend to have big budgets and big audiences, who already have some residual awareness. In this case, channel selection will be led by brand-building objectives, getting people to think and feel something, so they continue to choose that brand in the face of a constantly shifting set of interesting alternatives. Channel selection and budget are critical and need to be tightly matched to overall marketing strategy. There might be enough money to use TV (remembering that production spend will be higher than for most other channels) but perhaps not for long. Or the same budget might buy posters for an entire year but deliver a less rich and emotional message and perhaps only reach an urban audience. More established big brands will have data going back years to define the return they get from advertising in different channels, using statistical models (called econometrics) to help them understand what's the most efficient and profitable spend level for different channel mixes. There's a lot of data involved in this, but that doesn't make it entirely objective, as every player has prejudices about different channels, and the creative agency will have a view about what they really want to do for their idea, irrespective of what the data tells them.

The impact of advertising can often be hidden by other variables, when looking at the sales line alone. Thousands of dollars can be spent and even though nothing seems to happen to sales, the advertising may have been having a powerful effect that has been offset by other factors (competitive activity, retailer promotions, weather, seasonality, etc.). Econometric models help, though, by isolating the effect of advertising from these other variables (provided there is enough historical data to build such a model). Having models like this that reveal the true power of the investment is another advantage of being big when it comes to advertising.

The current available data suggests that the best strategy is to maintain some spend in market for as many weeks of the year as you can. Much like investing in the stock market, it's best to take a consistent long-term approach – the gains won't be immediately apparent, and you need to have enough capital to make the investment, but it will invariably pay back over time. To some it feels intuitive to gather lots of customers in a big launch and then let the product or service itself keep those customers loyal. Sadly, this loyalty is often an illusion, in a world of constant novelty and interesting new choices. Habit is a much more powerful force, as people do not like to think too much when making decisions, so finding ways to keep the brand top of mind for as long as possible is usually a good idea. No matter how exciting the advertising might be, everything is subject to decay in memory, so awareness will fade, although this may only matter if the objective is to build awareness.

If the objective is direct response, then it does not really matter how long a brand is advertising, as channels are planned for action rather than memory. The channel model keeps running and the rate of customer acquisition is monitored, along with channel response levels, which can vary dramatically over time. The best bet is usually to reach the audience as cheaply as possible in channels that enable them to respond fast (posters are probably not such a good choice in this scenario), and to adapt spend if response numbers go south. It is all about defining objectives clearly and then planning a channel mix to meet them.

**Key ideas:**

> Despite an almost infinite number of ways to reach people with a message, the most important goal is to reach as many people as cost-effectively as possible. Each channel has dramatically different attributes that must be taken into account when judging creative work.

*But maybe this is just an outmoded view; hasn't the internet changed everything?*

## Chapter 6

# How the internet is changing advertising

Most advertising that people have seen or heard recently was probably on their smartphone. The last thing they bought? Maybe that was bought with their smartphone too. And if it was a purchase of any size or significance, then they probably used their smartphone to research it, or compare prices to look for a better deal. It is hard to exaggerate the influence of the commercial internet on advertising (although many do). After years of rapid and accelerating change, the picture has cleared a little, the trends are more stable, enabling us to tiptoe through the hype and understand what's going on.

## The end of advertising?

The 'end of advertising', or perhaps even the 'end of brands' is a core hypothesis of many internet gurus. It comes from two pretty big assumptions, which are easier to believe if you work in tech and live in a US coastal city.

The first assumption is that the internet makes brands irrelevant, because it creates a state of almost perfect information. Brands were created when packaged-goods companies could control the narrative and add 'intangible value' to good-enough products by building an image, most powerfully through TV advertising, that enabled them to charge more. This also gave them leverage through big retailers, blocking out competition and dominating shelf space. The two factors together were the powerful forces that drove growth, initially in their home markets and then globally. Retail brands pulled off a similar trick by buying up available land for retail space and then using adspend to attract customers. The scale they achieved with space and spend gave them the market power to negotiate better prices from producers and pass those savings on to customers. Independent brands and independent retailers were rarely able to reach a profitable critical mass and struggled to raise the capital to survive.

The commercial internet changed all this, as people could find out about any product with just a click or two, so would not be hoodwinked by all that clever advertising. The growth of online retail makes retail chains irrelevant and shelf space an artefact of the past. You can have everything and anything you want, at the best price, wherever and whenever you like. There is simply no reason to care about brands, you just buy the best products and services. Instead of investing in brands and products, companies should invest in online distribution and inherent product quality. Everything else is simply the inefficiency of the market caused by imperfect information and the inconvenience of geography.

The idea of choosing what to buy at all may also become a thing of the past. We are moving to a sharing and subscription economy, where buying into a few core services can do all the choosing for people. Sign up to a few service providers and there is no need to ever go to a store ever again. All products will arrive automatically, and the money to pay for it will flow in and out of bank accounts (which may also automatically switch service provider if it spots a good deal).

The second assumption is that everyone will avoid advertising, as the ad-supported model of mass media collapses due to forces of supply and demand. On the demand side, people will simply stop watching commercial TV, choosing instead to watch everything on-demand via Netflix, Amazon Prime and other similar subscription streaming services (which will also mean that nobody wants to go to the cinema anymore). They will have no need for commercial radio because of Spotify. All the content anyone cares about from newspapers and magazines is available for free online, organised by Facebook, Google or Apple (and the bits that are not free will be subscribed to, without ads). Ad-blocking software means that nobody need see any ads online anyhow. Posters around town are probably unavoidable, but that is about it. The supply side of the equation will finish off any remaining advertising budgets, as those who previously advertised switch those budgets to building relationships with the online providers who are actually doing the choosing, reducing their prices and investing to make their products and services better. In a world where advertising has all but disappeared, there is obviously no need for advertising agencies.

These are almost plausible scenarios, and if you are reading this some years into a future where they have come to pass, you can marvel at my prescience. The only problem is quite how far these realities are from current experience (the latest UK report from 2019 shows that people spend almost ten times as much time watching traditional TV than they do watching streaming services or YouTube). Whilst big changes have happened in recent years that make us believe that anything could be possible, there is little evidence that most people want control of all the spending decisions in their lives ceded to Amazon. As for the end of brands, the fundamentals of how brands work really have not changed much – people tend to prefer to buy the biggest and most popular brands and feel that there is some value in design, image and the lifestyle associations they project to themselves and others (those who are the strongest advocates of the end of brands will often enthuse about internet start-ups, without fully realising the extent to which the brands of these start-ups have fuelled their enthusiasm – even a born-online start-up like Glossier says 'brand is everything'). Our brains are emotional decision makers and that will not change. Brands are here to stay. It is also worth thinking about how many of the purchase decisions you made recently were researched thoroughly or completed online. The answer will certainly be 'some' but almost certainly not 'all'.

The internet is not going to make brands disappear and is not likely to make advertising disappear (in fact at the moment it is proliferating both brands and advertising). But it has certainly changed advertising fundamentally and will continue to do so. The main change has been in the arrival of two of the most powerful companies the world has ever seen. In the 'end of advertising' scenario, neither one would exist any longer, because they are mainly funded by advertising and each now controls much more global adspend than any other company. This simple fact has caused some problems in commentary about changes in the industry, with some overstatement of their practical role as channels in any given market. For the first time, two entire channels are globally controlled by two single companies. If all the commercial TV stations in the world were run by just one company (or there were a local Facebook and Google in each country), then you would have a clearer and better debate about their real role and importance, but everything gets a little clouded by their global scale and stock price.

Of course, they are bigger than any TV company, but at the moment, as far as advertising is concerned, they are not bigger than all the TV companies. The other little mentioned fact is that their primary role (certainly in their years of fastest growth) has been to expand the market for advertising. The biggest single channel of advertising, even during the golden age of TV, was the classified section of newspapers – many small businesses and individuals, trying to get a message out there to someone, every day. It rarely touched advertising agencies and operated outside the advertising industry. It was a world of direct response rather than brand-building. This is currently the only channel that the internet has pretty much wiped out. Because in a world where Google exists, there is just no reason for it. The other growth has come from small businesses that would either never have needed to advertise in the past, or simply would not have existed in a world before the internet. For example, an independent restaurant would previously have attracted most of their diners from people walking past, or word-of-mouth recommendation. And nowadays, probably a fair chunk of their business still comes from that source. But if they don't also spend a little money on an online presence, they might as well not exist, because all the other restaurants in the area are tempting their customers away when they search 'restaurants near me' on their smartphone.

For millions of new small online businesses Google and Facebook have become their front door, as a shop on the high street would have been previously. They enable them to reach the entire world from their back bedroom, using the money that would in the past have been invested in rent (or perhaps in slowly and painstakingly building up a mailing list).

None of these businesses are individually spending very much on advertising. None of them would be worth an advertising agency's time. None of them would be worth Google or Facebook dealing with directly. But as simple, self-serve accounts that cost Google and Facebook virtually nothing to set up, they are worth dealing with. And there are millions of businesses like this, in every country in the world. And they are suddenly part of the ad industry. It is not a zero-sum game. The rise of Google and Facebook does not mean the fall of traditional media (even though journalists often portray it as such). Or at least not yet. The impact has so far been felt in a number of more subtle ways and we will consider each in turn.

## New channels

In the early days of the commercial internet, things were complicated. New attractions appearing all the time, many different advertising formats, a bewildering array of places to buy advertising from. Expertise was needed to navigate through all this. It gave birth to the first wave of digital agencies, who would take clients by the hand and help them with the complexity of this brave new world. What was good for these specialists was bad for the commercial development of the internet. The companies that would come to dominate advertising on the internet quickly realised that adspend would grow a lot faster if advertising online was simple and standardised, with platforms that enabled anyone to reach everyone. Specialist digital agencies still exist, although their reason to do so is now much more predicated on their ability to understand the 'culture' of advertising online and helping companies transform their own digital capability, rather than on their ability to navigate complexity. It is just not that complex anymore. Google and Facebook are the dominant players, so given that this is a short book about advertising, rather than a long book about the commercial internet, let us briefly look at how their platforms work.

Facebook is now one of the world's biggest and most profitable companies. Being so big and profitable also makes them a lightning rod for concerns about their effect on society. Facebook is the name of the company and also the name of one of their services, as Facebook owns Facebook, Instagram and WhatsApp. In most countries around the world (excluding China), these are all amongst the top five apps – for many people, Facebook is the internet, and their primary source of news and information about the world. We won't talk about WhatsApp much here, as it is currently not a platform where advertising can be paid for (although as the most popular messaging app, popular advertising content does get passed around and amplified here if people think it interesting enough to share). Both Facebook and Instagram share a similar business model: grow the number of users and grow the time each spends on it. It is called 'engagement' and has got Facebook into a fair bit of trouble. The logical end game (although they don't really talk about this) is for everyone to be using Facebook and spending all their time on the site. The more people use Facebook, the more incentive there is for others to use Facebook and the more Facebook learns about what each of them likes on Facebook. The business model demands that the Facebook algorithm gets really good at showing people things they like. Facebook maintains that they are a tech company, not a media channel, so have no responsibility for the quality, morality or veracity of that content. Whatever the user is into, Facebook will show them more compelling and more intensely interesting versions of that stuff, to keep them on the platform for as long as possible. What started out as just friends and family posting updates and photos has become a TV station, newspaper, shopping mall and social club all rolled into one, sitting in everyone's pockets.

Instagram began as a photo sharing platform and is still much more image-based than Facebook, but with increasing amounts of video. Facebook began as a place where people mainly connected with people they know; Instagram has always been a place where people follow those who produce attractive content, in addition to people they know. This has enabled the emergence of 'influencers', people whose content has its own audience, enabled by Instagram (more of this when we discuss YouTube later).

Both Facebook and Instagram work on a 'feed' system, where users 'scroll' to see new content (these apps are now so ubiquitous that most readers will be familiar with this already). When people spot something they like, they can pause and spend a little more time looking at it, or comment on it, like it or share it with others. There are lots of images, a fair bit of text and growing amounts of video. Ads can be bought within this 'feed', appearing in between the other content. Just as with that content, the user can choose to spend more time with the ad, or not. Much of it rushes past rather quickly, controlled by the user's interest, so when advertising is created for these platforms, the main thing is to attract attention quickly, so people pause to look. Compared to TV advertising, it is as though people are watching on fast forward, with their finger hovering over the play button just in case they see something they like. Even if they do pause, it's probably going to only be for a few seconds, so advertising on Facebook and Instagram is the art of economy. Striking images, tempting offers, bright colours. They are both very effective and very well-established platforms for direct-response advertising, especially if the products can then instantly be purchased online. Their effectiveness model for building brands in the long term is rather less clear, although studies in each platform will give you some rudimentary measures of awareness uplift.

When Facebook and Instagram began, brands took a few years to get to grips with how they worked. The initial idea was to 'be part of the community' and set up accounts that people might voluntarily follow or choose to be friends with. This really did seem like the end of advertising, because if people just reached out and welcomed brands into their lives, then nobody would have to pay to interrupt them in media. But perhaps unsurprisingly, it turned out that if you only communicated with people who invited you in, you ended up with a rather small audience. Some brands did work out how to create content for these channels so compelling and entertaining that they now spend very little on media (Red Bull is a good example of this, having become as much a broadcaster of extreme sports and music as they are a manufacturer of energy drinks). This is tough to do, and most brands do not succeed. Even those that do succeed tend to supplement this 'earned' exposure with advertising in paid media channels. Brands' presence on Facebook and Instagram is now largely conventional advertising, doing pretty much the same job, in the same way advertising has always done.

Google is a bit more complicated. For a start, we are actually talking about Alphabet, rather than Google, as that is the quoted entity. It seeks to distance itself from the Google search engine by renaming the company that owns it and a range of other ventures like Deep Mind and Waymo. For our purposes, we will not be looking at any of this, just Google's main advertising business. This splits into three areas – display, search and YouTube.

Google isn't the only provider of display advertising, but it is the biggest player. Various forms of display or 'banner' advertising have existed almost as long as the commercial internet. It works in a very similar way to newspaper advertising, but often with added video and animation to catch the eye. The creative considerations are similar to Facebook and Instagram, but with perhaps even less promise of actual attention, as the ad will never be the main thing people are looking at (even though it flies past at speed, there is at least a screen-filling moment in the Facebook or Instagram feed). There is also a third party involved – the site the ads are placed on. Display advertising enables publishers and news organisations to earn money from their online efforts (as so few are able to persuade people to pay) and Google's role in this (alongside other ad networks) makes selling this adspace very straightforward without them having to set up their own costly and complex ad sales operations.

Search is very different. Google is not the only search provider, but in most countries it has an almost total share of this market, and is the main gateway to the internet for most people. The critical thing about search is that it responds to users' intent. When they search for something, they are telling you what they want, at that moment. If an advertiser is looking for direct response, then this is a good time for them to show that person their ad. Typically, this is a text ad, appearing within or alongside the search results (everyone has used Google, so we do not need to explain what they look like). Sure, it is advertising, and accounts for a big chunk of Google revenue, but ad agencies normally have very little to do with it, as search is usually managed in-house or by the media agency. For many businesses that trade online (travel is a good example of a category that has moved almost entirely online in many countries; Booking.com is one of Google's biggest global spenders), this adspend can be their lifeblood, spending millions every month buying search ads alone. It is another good example of tech growing the advertising market. None of this is money that would previously have been spent in any of the previous forms of advertising. It is a new market catering to new possibilities.

And then there is YouTube. If Instagram was Facebook's smartest acquisition, then YouTube was Google's. A video sharing platform that contains a dizzying array of content from high definition Hollywood movies to the most trivial low-interest smartphone footage and everything in between. Like Instagram, it has enabled a new form of cultural expression, with 'influencers' able to post videos on their channels that are then immediately available to an audience that is potentially the entire world. YouTube sells video advertising; there are a range of formats, but often they depend on attracting the attention of an audience in the first few seconds so they choose to keep watching rather than skipping through to the video they really wanted to see. YouTube used to be entirely search driven – you look for something, you watch it. But it is increasingly working on an engagement-driven feed model now, especially in its dominant form as a smartphone app. You might choose your first video, but then YouTube auto plays another video it thinks you might like, and then another, then another, until you decide to stop. Much like Facebook and Instagram, it is a very compelling way to fill all those little boring parts of the day with a bit of entertaining distraction. For advertisers, it offers a way to keep video in the mix if you do not want to use TV. It is also used as a repository for all the video a brand might make, so suddenly every ad you ever made is available to anyone (which can cause problems if you made something embarrassing, as some brands have discovered to their cost). In a similar way to Facebook, many brands originally thought the way to do YouTube was to act like a content creator, make a channel and wait for people to beat a path to your door and watch those videos. Of course, for most brands this did not work very well (with a handful of notable exceptions), and YouTube has mainly become a conventional paid-for advertising channel.

## New ways to buy media

One of the most fundamental changes of advertising using these channels is how the media is traded, entirely facilitated by the possibilities of the technology. In conventional channels, even in the internet age, the channel itself is being sold, with a promise of an aggregated audience with certain characteristics. This audience is an estimate from research –

usually a very good estimate, but an estimate nonetheless. Advertisers are buying a typical audience for that programme, or publication, but do not know for sure if those were the people that actually watched when their ad appeared. And of course, they are buying the whole audience, not just the ones they want. For big brands, this is no problem, as their audience is probably everyone, so buying them as an aggregate is good value. But for smaller brands, or advertisers with a strong desire to avoid 'wastage' at all costs, then it is a problem. Facebook and Google are the answer to this problem, because on the internet, they sell the audience, not the show. The ads that any given individual sees when they watch YouTube are not the same ads someone else sees when they watch the same show on YouTube. The other big difference is that advertisers can buy this audience one by one, setting a defined budget that can either be capped or replenished. For small brands, this has been a gateway into sophisticated advertising strategies, on initially low budgets. Previously, chunks of money would have to be gambled all at once, now they can play their way in gradually, building a model of response and optimising as they go. It was an entirely new way to buy advertising. It works for Google and Facebook, having automated the process of selling these audiences to businesses (and the audiences can be very specifically defined, up to a point). The revolution has worked less well for conventional channels who still struggle to match this sales story.

It is a very compelling sell. But there are still question marks about value for money. Beyond online retail direct response, the effectiveness of these channels remains a little unproven, and the more specific brands get about their audience, the more it costs them to target each one of them. Eliminating wastage comes at a cost, compared to the bundled audiences you can buy in conventional media.

The other new way to buy 'media' through Facebook and Google is via direct partnerships with the aforementioned influencers. With creative that takes us back to the days when TV presenters would read out the ads during the programmes, many of these influencers will create 'native' content, where their endorsement of the brand is built into the content itself. Google and Facebook have created this possibility through the channels, although they do not tend to directly profit from these deals themselves. Often the deals are done directly between the brands and the influencer, with no media agency involvement. Podcasts also often work in this way, carrying advertising created by the podcaster, in the style of the show, rather than simply offering their audience for mass-produced creative that could run in any audio format.

## New creative possibilities

There is no doubt that internet culture has affected the way that advertising is created. YouTube in particular has enabled influences and film techniques to inspire more creative people more easily and quickly than was ever possible in the past (and sometimes this 'inspiration' goes all the way to copying, sometimes with the involvement of the original creator, sometimes without). It has enabled longer-form content to be made, with advertising sometimes simply being used to point at a YouTube link where the real creative work can be found and enjoyed, at a time length that would be prohibitively expensive to buy on TV. Sometimes this works, most often not, as the numbers of people who bother to follow the breadcrumbs to the longer content are very small. Why would they bother? It's just advertising after all. It has also changed the face of direct response – in the past, large chunks of any ad (time or space), would need to be devoted to getting people to write down or remember a phone number, or sometimes even an address. In a world with Google, people need only to remember your brand name and search can do the rest.

There is also the promise of data enabling personalised creative. On the internet advertisers are buying individuals rather than aggregated audiences; the core message can be adapted to appeal to each of those individuals, adapted to the things they like. The meaning of the brand can turn up in a variety of different guises, depending on how much is known about the person looking at the advertising. With digital outdoor, this approach can work on the streets, too, with advertising tailored for its location, or time of day (although the posters still do not know who is walking past, this is probably just a matter of time, as it would only need to sense the smartphones in the pockets of passers-by). The possibilities seem almost endless, although for brand com- munication it is not really clear whether a personalised message is more effective than a perfectly crafted broadcast message. And personalisation can start to feel a little creepy. People now largely know that data is being gathered about them all the time, but often do not want that fact to be made abundantly evident in every commercial message they see.

Even without personalised messaging, the data that can be gathered on the performance of different messages allows campaigns to be optimised in real time. Executions that perform better can be shown more, and those that perform worse can be taken out of the mix. This has a much more powerful effect if the role of advertising is to get people straight from the advertising to the retail destination. Direct response is much easier to measure, and many of the tech companies that advocate these data-driven methods of increasing efficiency cannot imagine any other form of advertising. Because that is how they built their business. The problem is that extensive studies of advertising have shown that the greatest benefits to a business are felt through brand-building in the long term (Les Binet and Peter Field have written extensively on this topic and produced a considerable body of evidence). There is no way of measuring which of a number of executional variants are doing this in the short term.

The greatest benefit of the internet for advertising creative is new possibilities of adaptation and responsiveness in the short term. The greatest casualty is the considerable profit advantages of a consistent long-term approach in a world where the constant flow of data seems constantly to demand action and change.

## New business models

The other significant new possibility offered by the internet is the ability to create brands with a totally new aesthetic and little or no media spend. These direct-to-consumer brands share a set of characteristics that were rare in the pre-internet world. Brands like Glossier, Warby Parker, Harrys, Casper and many more are often built on personal stories of the founders, a bright quirky design aesthetic, and sell to a 'community' rather than 'customers'. There is a sense of collective ownership for many of these brands, with the customers feeling like they have a personal relationship with the founders. These founders can be known purely through the brands they create, but they are also often 'influencers' from YouTube and Instagram, who then spin off passion projects into multi-million-dollar brands, based on their readily addressable audience. Communication is created to be shared, using the community to pass on the message to friends and family, fulfilling the 'death of advertising' hypothesis mentioned earlier. It may be that one day all brands are like this, and it becomes the dominant model for brands and communication. It is more likely that these brands will simply be part of many markets, mainly because building brands like this looks effortless, but is really, really tough to do. The effort or investment will have been put in somewhere, either in years of work building an audience as an influencer, or by spending big on advertising that does not look like big-spending advertising. For many existing brands, it has caused a search for authenticity, ensuring that what they actually do matches more closely with the claims they make, and a tone of voice in many communications that often feels more folksy than corporate.

### New problems

It is a brave new world, for sure, changing fast and offering many benefits. When the world's biggest and most successful companies of all time are in the vanguard, marketing people can look like quite the luddite if they are not jumping in with both feet. There is certainly a lot to like. And for the advertising industry, it has created many new ways to target people and to do our job better.

Digital channels are often not subject to the same kind of effectiveness scrutiny as other areas of advertising and business. Instead they have become a rather crude measure of modernity and progressiveness, a sense that really modern new companies spend all their advertising budget online and those that do not should be increasing the online percentage year on year. That is just nuts. In this rush to be modern, it is easy to forget a few crucial things.

The effectiveness model behind advertising on the internet is in its infancy. We know a lot about the channels that existed before and have a huge amount of data about how they work. Some of this data is less applicable nowadays, but the possibilities of these channels are well known and well practised. That is not true on the internet. There is a lot of data, but not many years of experience behind it. And the vast majority of advertising data is about direct response. For many years, Google and Facebook did not even really notice that there might be other reasons to make advertising, because as tech companies they lived in a culture where the only possible reason to advertise would be to get people to your site, now. They woke up to brand advertising, but then discovered that it was not easy to measure, and as a result still have not properly applied themselves to this task. You will get some rudimentary, in the moment ad diagnostics, largely based on short-term awareness lift, but these do not really answer the question. Much like the effects of Google and Facebook in general, they may be doing very powerful things, not all of which they intend, and not all of which are to the benefit of society and business, but it is just too early to understand them.

The regulatory framework around the internet is being built as we go and is nowhere near as well established as that which surrounds other channels, in most countries. A well-established regulatory framework builds trust, because people know that what they are seeing is broadly true and that consequences will occur if they are lied to. Online, it is a different matter. Of course, big brands will apply the same ethical standards to their online ads as they do to all their other work, but other companies will not. There is no pre-vetting, so advertisers of all kinds can say anything they like, and messages can only be taken down once they are seen and complained about. In many cases, advertising might look like opinion, or content or journalism, so the audience does not understand that there is intent behind the communication. And you do not know who is paying for it.

The same applies to the regulatory framework around the channels themselves. Newspapers, magazines and radio and TV stations have limits around the type of content they can show and a system to punish them if they infringe these limits. Because Google and Facebook will be very keen to tell you that they are tech companies, not media companies, they choose to take little responsibility for the content that users post and upload. They are just the platform, the responsibility lies with the user, and there is simply too much content being posted for them to look at it all and block the objectionable stuff. This may be bad for society as a whole. When that content is funded by ads, it is bad for brands. Whether to boycott YouTube or Facebook, or whether to pressure them to police their content more effectively, has become an urgent issue for business and government alike. It is hard to fix.

The internet so far has been very good for advertising and very good for brands. As it continues it may prove to be the death of advertising and the death of brands. It is changing everything in the industry, and yet much of the structure of the industry remains unchanged. For those who work in advertising nowadays, and in the coming years, it is the main force to manage. The trick is to understand the problems and not get carried away with the hype. The fundamentals have not changed, even though the channels have.

**Key ideas:**

In some ways the internet has changed everything about advertising, opening up new possibilities for ideas and their deployment. Many of these changes are still in their infancy with the possibility of even greater changes ahead. And yet in some ways, the internet has not changed the fundamentals in any way, as the main task of advertising remains to find a way to interrupt and distract people for long enough to deliver them a message.

*Advertising has not fundamentally changed then, but how does it work?*

**Chapter 7**

# How does advertising work?

Everyone has a view about advertising. People delight to tell stories about this or that advert they saw (almost always a TV ad, even now). 'It was that funny one, you know with the little cartoon animal, I love that guy, but I can't remember who it was for – so it can't have been very good!' People like to think that they know how their own brain works and can therefore understand when they're being persuaded and how. But unfortunately for them, that's not really how things work.

There are many different views, theories and models about how advertising works. At its simplest, money is spent on advertising and then a business or organisation comes out better than it would have done had that money not been spent. That result may be greater profits, greater revenue or mass behaviour change. Sometimes it's easy to see with the naked eye, other times it needs a bit of analysis to reveal itself (especially if competitors are doing the same thing, with more money).

The influence of advertising can be felt in a number of different ways. Advertising tends not to be a neat, single purpose tool, not a hammer for banging nails into a wall. The effects of advertising can be unpredictable and often only become apparent after the investment has been made. Sometimes the investment case needs to be tailored to how a very rational business thinks about advertising, whereas the smart advertising person knows that any single-use business case will almost certainly understate the effects. Here is just a flavour of the many ways advertising can work:

Advertising helps people remember brands, as they tend to choose what they know.

Advertising makes people feel more warmly towards brands, as they choose what they like.

Advertising gives people information, so they understand what is on offer.

Advertising makes things seem more popular as people like to do what others do.

Advertising influences behaviour, so people start to live their lives differently.

Advertising stops people changing, by reinforcing habit.

Advertising excites people by offering them novelty.

Many of the theories and models about how advertising works were developed before we knew very much about the brain. Knowing about how the brain works is fundamental to understanding how advertising works, because the brain is where advertising works. Even the most outdated, inaccurate, but surprisingly persistent models of thinking about advertising agree that it is intended to influence how we think.

The classic advertising effectiveness model is known as AIDA. It suggests, not unreasonably, that in order to buy, we progress through four distinct stages. The first is Attention – we must know that something exists before we can buy it, so the first job of advertising is to attract attention. Then comes Interest – we need to feel that the product or service has some relevance to us to get closer to purchase. Next is Desire – what benefit might this offer that may make our lives better? Finally, Action – information about how or where to get hold of the product or service and for this to be made simple and easy.

The origins of this theory go back more than a hundred years, the specific AIDA codification often credited to E. St Elmo Lewis. It is adapted from a process that at first seems superficially similar to the role of advertising, that of the door-to-door salesman (it was almost always a man), or commercial traveller, (as they were mysteriously referred to in Britain, where we consider 'selling' to be a rather vulgar and obvious thing to do). They would knock on doors and then run through a spiel that resembled the AIDA structure – the knock (Attention), an opening remark that made the householder think about whether they were really satisfied with how clean their carpets are, or whether or not their children were sufficiently well educated (Interest), then, often accompanied by visual aids, they painted a picture of the life of cleaner carpets, or children who ace their exams (Desire), followed by a reveal of the carpet cleaner or encyclopaedia that would make this possible at an enticing price (Action). It worked. Again and again in millions of households. The content and structure were refined and honed, and the feedback was immediate. Sales rose when it was delivered well and stalled when the formula was departed from. The people in charge of the sales force were then the people who began to be in charge of the advertising. Early advertising was either an enhancement of, or a replacement for, these door-to-door conversations, an automation and scaling up of the process. This was outlined by Claude Hopkins in his book *Scientific Advertising*, who thought of advertising in precisely this way.

This then led to a way of thinking about creating advertising that persists in many marketing departments and ad agencies today. The structure is: Insight, Benefit and Reason to Believe. The Insight is a 'mind-opening thought' that both demonstrates empathy into the lifestyle of the audience and makes them think about the imminent product or service in a different way. The Benefit can be rational, or emotional, sometimes both, but needs to make people feel that the thing being advertised is going to improve their life. Then the Reason to Believe is there to convince and close the deal, saying more about the ingredients that went into delivering this benefit, or the experts who endorse it. The advert is thus structured to convince the sceptical, hacking into their suspicious minds and seducing them.

It all makes perfect sense.

It all sounds very plausible.

But there are a number of problems with it.

It assumes that exposure to the advertising and the purchase of the product happen at virtually the same time. This of course is how it worked with door-to-door sales. An effective salesman knew that if he left the house without a commitment to purchase and an order in his hand, then his day was wasted. He had to work through the AIDA structure in a minute or two and then move on to knock on the next door. But that is not usually what happens with advertising, where exposure to the advertisement is usually some way away from the moment of purchase, either in time or physical distance. It also implies that advertising can only work through rational persuasion, that people need to make an active and rational decision before they buy (with a 'reason to believe').

Instead of solving these problems, the advertising industry first began to create a set of elaborate research tools to attempt to resolve this issue of memory. They got halfway to the right solution in identifying that they needed somehow to address the time lag between exposure to advertising and subsequent purchase. These research tools (still widely used) measure how well people consciously remember your advertisement – they would be asked if they could remember seeing any ads in a particular category (for an insurance company, a car, a fruit juice, etc.) and then whether they could remember seeing any ads for a particular brand. Finally they would be shown the ad in question and asked whether they had seen it before. Memory of this type is very unreliable (you will get lots of false positives, where people think they have seen your ad but have not and lots of false negatives where people have seen the ad but cannot consciously remember having done so).

We now know a lot more about how the brain makes decisions and stores memories, but this has mostly not changed the way we try to measure advertising. We are still in thrall to recall and recognition. The evidence suggests that recall and recognition has very little to do with effectiveness, but everyone wants to be noticed and remembered, right? Why would that be a bad thing? And when given a 'score' of some sort, however irrelevant, there is an instinctive urge for that score to be higher than everyone else's score. So, we chase these rather irrelevant metrics. This has not deterred the research industry (and indeed many people who work in advertising), who continue to reinforce the idea that advertising needs to be noticed, and that good advertising 'stands out'. Many will give you data about the number of commercial messages we see in a day and how few we recall – with the implication that the goal is to be one of those few that are recalled. If that was the case, then the advertising industry would have collapsed long ago, as it would have been like selling chocolate bars where only one in a thousand packets actually contained chocolate. It is seductive for clients when creatives talk to them about the mass of advertising messages we see every day and that a mere handful are remembered, because it suggests that both client and agency are excellent and talented enough to 'win' this race for attention. It is quite exciting, but rather irrelevant. Because if advertising really did work like that, 99% of it would be a waste of money, and businesses would find a more useful thing to do. It is probably the case that almost all advertising works at some level, precisely because it does not have to be noticed to work (unless the role of advertising is for people to act there and then).

As we got to know the brain better, we began better to understand memory and decision-making. The work of Daniel Kahneman (best known from his book *Thinking Fast and Slow*) has been extraordinarily influential here, with Robert Heath applying the theory to the practice of creating advertising (in his book *Seducing the Subconscious*) and Byron Sharp (*How Brands Grow*) adding large empirical data sets to explore and codify the effect of doing so in market. In short, we now know a lot more about how advertising works and why (even though we still routinely use the language and metrics of attention and rational persuasion).

The truth is both faintly unpalatable and wonderfully liberating.

Real-world decisions are not made rationally by a

calculating and conscious brain. Every decision we make is filtered through the most primitive, emotional, instinctive part of the brain. We might talk ourselves into it, or post-rationalise it afterwards, but every decision we make is either entirely or partly emotional. For highly intelligent and analytical businesspeople, then this can be a bit hard to swallow, but it is true. What the brain wants to do is to conserve energy, and it does this by making the less important decisions in life automatically. Thinking hard about something and considering new information is sometimes necessary, but tiring, so when possible, we try to avoid those situations. We try to make as few considered, rational decisions as we possibly can, certainly not about things we buy often. The goal of marketing and advertising is to get people to think about the brand as little as possible, and for it instead to become part of automatic habit. For the ego-driven, extrovert people that populate advertising agencies and marketing departments this is somewhat counter-intuitive and rather disappointing.

Memories are stored either in the short term or the long term. Our brains are able to make a conscious effort to store complex new information and detail but often these things do not stick around for long. They are held for as long as needed and then forgotten. Longer term memories are made of simple emotional, instinctive associations. The brain is constantly taking in this kind of information, whether you like it not, and often you are not conscious of it happening. This automatic memory gets stored and sticks around. These are the memories that are most useful for brands and advertising: long-term emotional associations, built and reinforced over time. Advertising is just absorbed by the brain at this constant low level, as we pass through the world. It is not conscious and is impossible to stop (unless you never come into contact with any advertising at all). People do not like this idea very much. It makes advertising sound sinister and underhand, as it bypasses rational thought. But this is not a nefarious characteristic of advertising, it is an inconvenient characteristic of the brain. As we have previously discussed, advertising is often trying to be noticed, and work out in the open, but the brain is not very co-operative in this endeavour as it does not want to notice it.

Heath illustrates this with an example from UK car advertising. The most successful campaign of the time was for the Renault Clio, which included very little rational information about the vehicle, but instead built an association with playful Frenchness with stories of a father and daughter who used the sporty Clio to each conduct their own clandestine romances. Not a good rational reason to spend thousands of pounds on a car, but a very effective brand advertising campaign creating intangible emotional associations.

Byron Sharp's work went even further to define the creation of associations like this as the entire purpose of advertising and the reason *Why Brands Grow* (the title of the single most influential work on marketing and advertising in recent years). The book describes how advertising creates 'mental availability' by using 'distinctive assets' (shapes, colours, characters, celebrities, slogans) consistently over time to create simple and easily retrievable associations around brands. The goal is not for people to remember the advertising, the goal is to make the brand easy to choose and buy. This race is won by the brands that help the brain do as little work as possible. The most famous brands (not necessarily the brands with the most famous adverts) sell more and grow faster. It is not about being unique, or persuasive, it is about being consistent and creating an attractive image.

Sharp's work suggests there is a particular dividend to be gained from fame. Being the best known usually goes hand in hand with being the most used, and the most used is usually the most successful (it is possible to get success by securing a lot of spend from a small number of customers, but it is rare – Sharp's research demonstrates that most brands grow by getting more customers than other brands). You can debate chicken and egg here (does the awareness actually follow the usage, rather than the other way round?), but data from multiple sources shows that brands protect and grow their market share by spending at or above their share of market. The formula is SOV > SOM, share of voice calculated by adding up all the advertising spending in the market, across all channels, and then working out what percentage of that is accounted for by the advertising spend for any particular brand (in most countries, this data is available through syndicated market research companies). If share of spend is consistently greater than share of market, then growth will tend to follow.

But of course, this is not the whole story.

The picture of how advertising works is completed with the work of Les Binet and Peter Field, who resolve the contradictions between the short-term and long-term view of how advertising works. They analysed hundreds of campaigns that have documented effectiveness in the world's most rigorous effectiveness awards scheme (the IPA Effectiveness Awards). Those that do best combine long-term and short-term approaches (typically spending 60% on the former and 40% on the latter). Advertising works in both ways, to try to influence people to do something right now, by engaging the active part of the brain (although probably not in quite as rational and analytical a way as some of the early theorists believed) and also by engaging longer term memories to influence feelings over time, largely through the subconscious.

Both long-term and short-term matter are related to one another. If the long term is nurtured, then advertising with short-term goals becomes more and more effective over time. It requires faith, capital and patience to persist with long-term brand build, when the effect does not appear for months. But there is now a wealth of data behind this approach, so it requires less blind conviction and simply the application of this thinking to a business.

Paul Feldwick, in his book *The Art of Humbug*, has suggested a number of other ways in which advertising can work, different ways of thinking about both the short term and the long term. Unlike a mathematical formula, there is always more than one plausible answer. All of these different ways of working coexist at the same time, interacting with a number of other functions of a business to help produce returns:

Advertising as salesmanship (working to rationally convince).

Advertising as seduction (making a brand feel emotionally attractive).

Advertising as salience (just building and maintaining brand awareness).

Advertising as social connection (where popularity becomes a reason to buy in itself).

Advertising as spin (creating news and inspiring coverage beyond paid media).

> Advertising as showbiz (providing branded
> entertainment to attract attention).

Much like many theories in many fields, in some ways it does not matter which of these are deployed, as long as the decision is made deliberately, with an awareness of the strengths and weaknesses of the approach and the fit to the business. A rational, risk-averse business is unlikely to prosper by choosing the 'showbiz' model, as attracting attention often requires risk-taking. Similarly, an organisation driven by flair and emotion may struggle with salesmanship.

Broadly, advertising works by persuading that a product or service is better, so it is bought there and then; advertising also works by making brands famous, so people continue to buy them without thinking very much about it, for emotional, not rational reasons.

Has the advent of the internet changed this? Probably not, in that human brains have not changed (don't believe the hype about the internet rewiring our brains and attention spans, that's just short-term behaviour, not a fundamental change to brain function). There has been a shift to the direct model of advertising when creating work for online, partly because it's so easy to measure and partly because it worked for a lot of the early growth companies online, so it helped establish the template encouraged by Facebook and Google. Online purchase journeys have perhaps changed some of the dynamics of purchase, with the primary change being to collapse the geographic and temporal distance between ad exposure and purchase. But most people are online to enjoy community with friends or entertaining content, they are not just tapping or clicking on everything they see. It is much more likely that when they see advertising alongside the thing they are mainly looking at, it gets logged in their brain in the same way as a poster on the street and then it comes back to them when they are making a decision about a brand in that category. Simple and consistent associations that lead to easy decision-making.

This pull to the short term does seem to have been to the detriment of effectiveness. The latest research from Binet and Field has identified a dip in the effectiveness of campaigns featured in creative awards. The advertising industry is understandably keen to demonstrate modernity in the face of a rapidly changing world, but as a result a lot more short-term work has been created (because that has been the dominant mode of online advertising), with effectiveness suffering as a result, as long-term brand-building is neglected. This may change in future, but if the trend continues, advertising will become a less profitable activity for business.

If we know all this about how advertising works, then it is reasonable to think that research might be able to help predict which adverts will work best. Indeed, part of the approach to making advertising that works is using research to check messaging before media money is spent (it is customary to spend 10x as much on media as is spent on producing the advertising, so the media money is the bigger bet). Advertising research is a massive adjacent industry in its own right, with research agencies often owned by the same companies that own the ad agencies. Doing research on advertising is very popular amongst client companies (as their money is most at risk), although none of it can predict with too much certainty what works and is often based on models of advertising effectiveness that are very different from those used by the agencies who made it, and the marketing departments that bought it. Very few people seem at all concerned about resolving this contradiction. That is because a lot of advertising research is not really being done to make it work better, it is being done to justify decisions within organisations, enabling money to be secured or agreements to progress. It is very hard to be honest about this and still function, so we all pretend things are fine and keep moving forward.

Qualitative research, (often colloquially known as 'focus groups') is typically used in the early stages, when ideas are rough and still in development. Generally, sample sizes are small, but ideas can be explored a bit more thoroughly. The main problem is that looking at ideas in research groups is not very much like seeing advertising out in the real world. Research respondents pay much more attention, and as a result usually over-rationalise their reactions. Most of what is going on is about the social context of the group, with people looking to please the researcher, or impress the other respondents. Qualitative research can provide valuable learning, but only when the drawbacks of the method are taken into account.

Quantitative research involves talking to many more people, at a much later stage of the process, when many decisions have already been taken about what kind of advertising will be produced and which idea is favoured. The objective is usually to know how likely it is to work (or to provide that data to the boss). Companies that make a lot of advertising will invest very heavily in quantitative research, particularly if the advertising is going to run all over the world, as the cost of testing is dwarfed by the cost of media. Most quantitative methods (and there are a few) involve creating a test version of the ad (and it is usually a TV ad – there are very few established methods to test ideas that are not presented in this form). This piece of stimulus material is then shown to a few hundred, or a few thousand people who are asked questions about it. These questions vary by supplier, but they are usually intended to measure communication, persuasion, and potential recall. Each provider will have a slightly different spin on the method, some attempting to introduce more 'real-world' conditions by checking if respondents remember the ad some days after the test itself, or introducing questions that seek to understand their emotional response, or speed of reaction to the questions. There are now also pseudo-neuroscience methods that try to measure brain activity when watching advertising, or understand which bits of the advert are more or less interesting (although simply measuring brain activity does not actually tell you very much). Because they test a lot of advertising, most of the big providers will give you a one-number score, or a colour-coded dashboard that tells you where your ad sits versus all the others they have tested. Some client companies take these scores very seriously, using them to determine levels of media investment, and even salaries and bonuses for the marketing people involved in creating them.

There are a number of problems with this kind of quantitative pre-testing, the main one being that it has very little to do with how advertising actually works. The testing environment, by necessity, involves people paying a lot more attention to advertising than they ever would in the real world. And as with qualitative research, their answers are heavily over-rationalised. Many of the research companies will show charts with performance in pre-testing tracked against sales performance, or actual awareness build when the advertising runs. It is seductive but riddled with even more problems. You never find out about the false negatives in the testing (ads that would have been great in market, but scored badly) because very few of them run – the test stops them at development stage, so they are not in the data. And those ads that score well in pre-testing often build the confidence of the organisation, and increase the media investment, so the test itself has then contaminated the real-world deployment of the ad. And the correlations between test scores and real-world performance are often not that strong, with big outliers (ads that should have done well but did not, or ads that performed in market far better than their score suggested). This does not mean that quantitative testing is useless, just that it should be used cautiously and understood for what it really is. Complex organisations need tools to speed decision-making, or they can be stuck with inaction, subjectivity and politics. A number ratified by a multinational research company can go a long way to get things moving.

This type of testing also points to an important difference between clients and agencies around how they want advertising to work. Agencies are looking for outliers, exceptional one-offs that produce extraordinary spikes of interest and break the model. There is often a proud moment in award-winning case study videos, where agencies will proudly announce that the stores sold out of the product, or the brand's website crashed under the weight of excited traffic. This is the point where agencies high-five, open the champagne and take the rest of the day off. The client, however, is horrified, having just incurred the wrath of all their production and ops and tech people by failing to accurately forecast demand and having lost millions in potential sales. They are much more interested in a smooth upward curve, that is driven by slightly above-average advertising, of the type that a pre-testing model can often pick up. By definition, the model-breaking dramatic outliers won't be picked up by the model. Most clients are happy with that, because these unicorns create as many problems as benefits. Agencies find this very hard to understand.

Advertising works in hidden and subconscious ways, to an unquantified degree that research usually fails to predict and can only really be discerned accurately after millions of dollars have been spent on media. The kind of advertising that can be accurately measured upfront will often achieve much lower return on investment but be much more popular with the business. Advertising works. But it is not at all simple.

**Key ideas:**

Our understanding of how advertising works has increased over the years and evolved from rational to more emotion-based thinking. Effectiveness can be considered in terms of short-term sales activation and long-term brand-building with most successful advertising achieving both. Research is often used to develop and optimise ideas.

## If advertising works, then is this good or bad for us?

## Chapter 8

# Is advertising good or bad for us?

As long as advertising has been around, critics of advertising have existed. Most societies seem to acknowledge these potentially damaging effects by placing some limits on advertising, regulating how much of it can be shown and where, along with mechanisms for ensuring that it is legal, honest and truthful.

The fear of advertising began in the psychology era, immediately post-war. When advertising seemed to be little more than the product and its benefits writ large in bright colours, few worried too much about it. Or at least their worries were about the product or the service, or capitalism in general, rather than the discipline of advertising itself. There was some concern about the public sphere being despoiled by excessive commercial messaging (in its most rudimentary form, people disliked tradespeople shouting in the street), but this was quickly resolved with legislation defining limits on where and when advertising could appear. In the 1950s, something new happened. Rather than simply talking about the benefits of the product, brands were attached to lifestyles, in mass communication. This was the age when supply of goods began to outstrip demand in many rich countries (a totally unprecedented situation up to this point), and the customer had the luxury of choice, so advertising had to adopt new tactics to attract them to one brand or another, rather than just the category. Typically, the lifestyles on offer were polished and idealised, an ideal family, ideal mother, ideal man, ideal woman, ideal child. The almost certainly unintended effect of this type of advertising is to make people feel that their life is not good enough. They do not seem as happy as the people in the adverts, so there must be something wrong with them. The advertising suggests that if they had that product, the entire lifestyle associated with it might magically become theirs. So, they spend money they cannot afford on a product that does not really exist and when the lifestyle fails to arrive, they blame themselves and do it all over again. This process began in the psychology era, as many prominent followers of Freud arrived in the US advertising industry and purported to help agencies devise just the right signals to make people crave the associations with the brand or product. Many of these people promoted not only the products, but also themselves, becoming well known in their own right, and often claiming miraculous success for the businesses they worked with. This was a perfect combination of clever, sinister foreigners apparently employing sinister forces to manipulate the behaviour of credulous ordinary folk. They were not academics subjecting their work to rigorous peer review, but instead had a vested interest in appearing mysteriously powerful, as they were selling themselves as hard as they were selling their clients' products. It is hard to know whether they really were creating deleterious effects on the population, but people were certainly keen to believe that this might be the case. We often have a fascination with mysterious hidden forces, and advertising at this point fit the bill, with the magicians even publishing their books of magic for all to read.

The criticism that has persisted since this era is revealing, as it focuses on the idea of aspiration itself, and only really for people who were seen not to have enough money to make mistakes in this way. This is a possibly patronising regard for the welfare of the gullible masses, who are apparently not smart enough to see through the tactics of the advertisers and make their own decisions. Many of the critics would rather they aspired to different or better things and point out that people in these capitalist aspirant societies are no happier, and often much less happy than those in the old communist world, or primitive peoples who live simpler lives in poorer countries. The fact that this angst has now moved to Instagram, with a concern about the projection of idealised lives there leading to sadness and depression, is instructive. It partly indicates that advertising has moved on – the general mode of expression of advertising in more affluent countries is more often abstract or realist than idealised, so advertising is often not portraying any particular lifestyle. It also shows that the sense that others are having a better time (rather than accepting that everyone has problems and that there are no quick fixes), is a permanent feature of the modern human condition, rather than a particular symptom of advertising.

A secondary concern around the effect of advertising on society is related to the more recently arrived ad-funded platforms, particularly Facebook, Instagram and YouTube. Their ad-funded model drives them to try and keep people on their platform for as long as they can, as often as they can. This is achieved algorithmically, by showing people more and more of the things they seem to like. As has been well documented, this can lead to pockets of very extreme views and behaviours emerging, as well as creating a model for subverting democracy by giving lies and conspiracy theories the chance to solidify and propagate. It does not matter whether something is true, it just matters whether people seem to want to spend time with it. If the platforms were not ad funded, then this impetus would be much diluted, and these effects on society and politics far weaker. The advertising industry is certainly in some way responsible, as without it, these platforms would simply not exist.

Internet culture is the source of another criticism of advertising from a very different source. Many internet thinkers and evangelists of online business models cast advertising as an anachronistic pre-internet inefficiency. It is a cost that a smart modern business should not have to bear. And it will shortly be rendered totally ineffective, as the industry collapses now that the prevalence of smartphones has put perfect information in everyone's hands. The current growth of the advertising industry and future projections seem to suggest this news is fake, but nowadays we are permanently just around the corner from another startling discontinuity, so there may be a cliff edge awaiting. It is a fairly narrow view of the role of advertising as simply about information distri-bution, even though this is probably the least important and least lucrative aspect of advertising. And it narrowly defines the advertising industry as simply about interruptive paid media. Nowadays, advertising can add value in many more places, building that elusive (and perhaps illusory) emotional value for the brand. It is hard to measure, of course, but that does not mean it does not exist.

Even if advertising is delivered via Instagram rather than in a magazine, it is still advertising, and most evidence suggests that it adds value to businesses and brands, not just cost. Of course, it is possible, or maybe even probable, that bad advertising drains cost from a business, but there is nothing about advertising in general that should do so. Bad practice is bad for business, whether applied to advertising, procurement, operations or finance.

Many countries around the world do seem to tacitly acknowledge that advertising is not a universally good thing, by subjecting it to regulation and restriction. Too much advertising, in too many places, too often, is not good for advertising, the media it appears in, or society in general. Efforts are made to protect children from certain kinds of advertising (often high-fat, salt and sugar food and drink), to clip the wings of messaging and distribution for other kinds of advertising (alcoholic drinks can often only be advertised at certain times of day, in certain channels, and with stringent restrictions on messaging) and to ban advertising for certain products altogether (tobacco and cigarettes fall into this category in many countries, although not all, and prescription pharmaceuticals are similarly restricted although not in the world's biggest advertising market, the US). This suggests that advertising does have the capacity to be bad for us. This malign influence is wrapped up in an acknowledgement of the power of advertising and the limits of capitalism in general. Market forces left un-checked, amplified by advertising, can lead us down dark paths. This understanding might be linked to the advertising industry's desire to give itself awards for good works, with a disproportionate amount of the industry awards going to charitable efforts of one sort or another, as though the industry was trying to atone for sins elsewhere.

As with many things in life, it is about getting to the right balance. Properly regulated advertising causes little widespread harm, does some good and helps businesses and brands flourish. Making this case has been strangely problematic for the advertising industry. When we look at how the industry promotes itself, the tactic is often to point at advertising done in the public sector or for charities (this kind of work is disproportionately represented in creative awards) and campaigning for as little regulation as possible. This is neither a particularly credible argument (advertising done for charities makes agencies very little money, so the industry would collapse if this were the primary activity), nor the strongest argument that could be made. Advertising contributes to the success of businesses, and is a thriving industry in its own right, contributing to economic growth. Economic growth is the most reliable way to improve living standards, advance healthcare and medical science and lift people out of poverty. Making advertising for medical or poverty charities is a much less efficient way to make the world better than making effective advertising for commercial organisations that employ many people and pay their taxes. The core business of advertising is good and worthwhile for everyone if done well and properly regulated.

In the broader advertising industry, this desire to be seen to 'make the world better' is currently manifest through the desire to define and communicate your brand's 'purpose'. This purpose is often defined in terms that make you wonder whether this is a commercial organisation at all (Google's is famously 'to organise the world's information and make it universally accessible and useful', even though the real purpose of organising this information is to organise the world's eyeballs and make them commercially useful and lucrative for advertisers). Global multinationals like Unilever are attempting to define this higher social purpose for each of its brands and, if it cannot be done, to divest those brands that are not sufficiently purposeful. There is some evidence that global consumers are now much more interested in whether companies are behaving properly, with the threat of climate change and a growing awareness of how poorly some companies treat their workers. Whether communicating their desire to solve these problems is either the best use of advertising or the best justification for advertising's positive influence in the world is open to question. When used as a distraction by companies who are not actually doing enough real change on the real issues it is probably evidence that advertising is not good for society.

The advertising industry's own actions seem to point to ethical misgivings about their own industry. Each year the industry gathers in Cannes, in the south of France to award the work they consider to be the best, from across the world. Awards have always played a big role in advertising agencies, helping build careers and promote what the industry is capable of. There has even been a compelling link made between the most awarded work and gains in effectiveness, so it is not just a self-indulgence. But if you spend any time in Cannes you quickly see that a huge proportion of the awards are given to charity, public sector or cause-related campaigns. Often quite low budget and nowadays often tech enabled, this speaks to an industry that wants to be doing 'good' in the world, seeking legitimacy by promoting the work it does for charity rather than embracing the commercial imperatives that drive the bulk of any advertising agency's revenues.

Advertising is good for us if you believe that business is good for us, whatever the industry might want you to believe about its work with charities. The effect on the economy is the main thing, because when we are all richer, we're generally all better off.

**Key ideas:**

The debate will always rage as to whether advertising is an evil force persuading us to buy things we don't need or a positive driver of economic growth. 'Do more good than harm' might serve as a good rule of thumb.

## Afterword

# Does advertising have a future?

The advertising industry as we once knew it is gone forever.

The profit margins that were once available have become unsustainable, and agencies are in many ways tougher places to work than they were in the old days. The energy in the financial markets has moved away from the global advertising holding companies and towards tech companies. When it became clear that the internet would come to dominate advertising, these global holding companies could have attempted to reinvent themselves as tech companies, but they chose not to (and their investors would probably have been unhappy with the vast investment that would have been required). Instead we have an industry that has become a tech follower, not a tech leader, chasing after the global behemoths that dominate standards and trading systems in the way that agency groups used to. Clients increasingly look over the table at their agencies wondering whether they are the partners they need to thrive in the future, perhaps unconvinced by a creative product that in many ways is indistinguishable from that produced twenty, thirty or even forty years ago.

And yet, of the five biggest companies the world has ever seen, three (Alphabet, Facebook, Amazon) are either entirely or partly advertising firms. Each individually has a value that dwarfs that of the entire advertising industry of previous generations. This valuation assumes tremendous growth in coming years. Yes, they are not creative agencies, and they do not buy media, but they are the advertising industry. It is how they grew, and they would struggle to survive without advertising as their business model. The fundamental needs of brands and businesses have not changed – they need to be known by potential customers and they profit by building intangible associations beyond their functional delivery. Advertising is good at both of those things.

The future of the advertising industry will not involve someone sitting in an office writing a TV script or sketching out a poster before retiring to a long boozy lunch. It will be about data, it will be about complexity, it will be about strategy and intelligence, but above all it will be about creativity. However it is deployed, this creative ability to make people think and feel differently about a product or service, which might in itself not have changed at all, is a type of business alchemy. Words and pictures that make people want to be part of something, that mean people enjoy things more than they otherwise would, that make the cost of every one of its component parts deliver more profit than they did before. The right words and pictures cost no more than the wrong ones, so this extra value is delivered for essentially nothing, making companies more valuable, and careers more successful. It is not what management consultancy does, it is not what data science does and it is not what coding does; it is different and special, and it works.

There has never been a worse time for advertising.

There has never been a better time for advertising.

CPSIA information can be obtained
at www.ICGtesting.com
Printed in the USA
BVHW070712060822
643966BV00008B/1271

9 781789 631937